A native of Romania, Mircea Eliade was educated at the universities of Bucharest and Calcutta. He has taught at universities throughout Europe and at the University of Chicago, where he is now Sewell L. Avery Distinguished Service Professor, History of Religions, and Professor, Committee on Social Thought.

He was President of the American Society for the Study of Religions from 1963 to 1967, and he is the author of many books, among them *Shamanism*, *Cosmos and History*, *From Primitives to Zen*, and *The Quest*.

SYMBOL, MYTH, AND RITUAL

Series Editor: Victor Turner

AUSTRALIAN RELIGIONS

An Introduction

AUSTRALIAN RELIGIONS

An Introduction

MIRCEA ELIADE

Cornell University Press

ITHACA AND LONDON

Chapters 1–5 are reprinted from *History of Religions,* Vols. VI (1966) and VII (1967), by permission of The University of Chicago Press. Copyright © 1966, 1967 by The University of Chicago.

International Standard Book Number 0-8014-0729-x
Library of Congress Catalog Card Number 72-6473

Printed in the United States of America by York Composition Co., Inc.

Librarians: Library of Congress cataloging information
appears on the last page of the book.

Foreword

Recently both the research and theoretical concerns of many anthropologists have once again been directed toward the role of symbols—religious, mythic, esthetic, political, and even economic—in social and cultural processes. Whether this revival is a belated response to developments in other disciplines (psychology, ethology, philosophy, linguistics, to name only a few), or whether it reflects a return to a central concern after a period of neglect, is difficult to say. In recent field studies, anthropologists have been collecting myths and rituals in the context of social action, and improvements in anthropological field technique have produced data that are richer and more refined than heretofore; these new data have probably challenged theoreticians to provide more adequate explanatory frames. Whatever may have been the causes, there is no denying a renewed curiosity about the nature of the connections between culture, cognition, and perception, as these connections are revealed in symbolic forms.

Although excellent individual monographs and articles in symbolic anthropology or comparative symbology have recently appeared, a common focus or forum that can be provided by a topically organized series of books has not been available. The present series is intended to fill this lacuna. It is designed to include not only field monographs and theoretical and comparative studies by anthropologists, but also work by scholars in other disciplines, both scientific and humanistic. The appearance of studies in such a forum encourages emulation, and emulation can produce fruitful new theories. It is therefore our hope that the series will serve as a house of many mansions, providing hospitality for the practitioners of any discipline that has a serious and creative concern with comparative symbology. Too often, disciplines are sealed off, in sterile pedantry, from significant intellectual influences. Nevertheless, our primary aim is to bring to public attention works on ritual and myth written by anthropologists, and our readers will find a variety of strictly anthropological approaches ranging from formal analyses of systems of symbols to empathetic accounts of divinatory and initiatory rituals.

The series begins with two books on the culture of the Australian aborigines. One is by an anthropologist, Nancy Munn, who is working on the frontiers of her discipline. She provides a "generative" account of the structure of the graphic sign system of a specific society, the Walbiri, explaining how its elements and combinatorial rules are employed to generate a potentially unlimited set of specific designs, each with its unique meaning. She examines the ways this sign system is utilized in different kinds of cultural contexts within the same society.

The other volume, Mircea Eliade's, presents a striking contrast in perspective, method, and data, for it is phenomenological, comparative, and based on written sources. It provides an example of the approach to religious systems that has been developed by the burgeoning discipline known as history of religions, and indeed its author is that discipline's most distinguished exponent.

Eliade offers an explicit critique of "the religious illiteracy of so many writers on primitive religions" and argues for the historicity of "primitive" religions against both the evolutionists and the romantic decadentists who see developments of religions as a linear movement from the simple to the complex, the former as going "up," the latter "down."

The chapters that follow apply these and other approaches to the data on Australian aboriginal religions— their High Gods, Culture Heroes, initiation and death rites, and medicine men. Eliade handles the classical sources with a historian's balanced judgment and culls the riches of the best modern authorities, including the Berndts, Elkin, Stanner, and Petri. Using these data, he moves through inference to hypothesis and detects the presence of certain patterns of ritual and belief that recur in Australian religions across the continent. Like the anthropologist Radcliffe-Brown (whose lectures "The Cosmology of the Australian Aborigines," delivered at University College, London, just after World War II, were among the decisive formative influences on my own career), he relied on intuition to discover general structures and configurations. And while it is easy to argue that the data on which these structures are based are not grounded on scientific methods of controlled comparison and quantification, better data are now impossible to obtain. Models and metaphors are coming to be regarded, as Max Black predicted a decade ago, a reputable part of scientific culture: "For science, like the humanities, like literature, is an affair of the imagination."[1]

Eliade stresses that the discovery of influences from

---

[1] Max Black, *Models and Metaphors* (Ithaca: Cornell University Press, 1962), p. 243.

Melanesia and other parts of Southeast Asia, as well as from more remote areas such as India, has destroyed forever the simplistic evolutionist notion of the truly "primitive" *Naturvolk* character of Australian religions, citing impeccable archaeological and linguistic evidence. His own vast scholarship in Eastern religion and Siberian shamanism enables him to put in sound comparative perspective his findings about initiation rites and secret cults.

"The ultimate goal of the historian of religions," Eliade writes in the concluding paragraph of this book, "is not to point out that there exist a certain number of types or patterns of religious behavior, with their specific symbologies and theologies, but rather to *understand their meanings.* And such meanings are not *given* once and for all, are not 'petrified' in the respective religious patterns, but rather are 'open,' in the sense that they change, grow, and enrich themselves in a creative way in the process of history."

He makes a signal contribution to the problem of the relationship between religion and historical processes, particularly with reference to modern religious movements, such as the Kuràngara cult, which spread through many Australian groups and which, for him, demonstrate the creative potential some religions exhibit in a spiritual crisis. Such movements generate symbols and rituals, and it is to these products of religious change that Eliade looks most attentively for indications of meanings in religions, for what Clifford Geertz has called "metasocial commentary."[2]

VICTOR TURNER

University of Chicago

[2] Clifford Geertz, "Deep Play: Notes on the Balinese Cockfight," *Daedalus*, Winter, 1972, p. 26.

Contents

Preface

At the end of his brilliant essay "On Understanding Non-Christian Religions," Ernst Benz explained why he coveted a "clear insight into the earlier stages of the religious consciousness of mankind." He desired to know "the way in which man has passed through these stages up to the present and how they lie submerged in the depths of our humanity in some form that is now barred and veiled from us. This is not the same as the desire to return to these stages. It is rather a wish to know the inner continuity of meaning in the development of the varied forms and stages of religious consciousness."[1] By "Non-Christian Religions" Benz was referring to Oriental and Far Eastern religions: Islam, Hinduism, Buddhism, Confucianism, Shinto. All these Asiatic traditions are ranged by Western scholars among the "high religions." With exemplary lucidity and candor Benz relates some of his main difficulties while trying to grasp the meaning of their symbols, rituals, or dogmas. Notwithstanding such experiences, many Western scholars think that important progress has been made in the last two generations, that thanks to the works of L. Massignon, G. Tucci, P. Mus, Ed. Conze, H. Corbin, D. T. Suzuki, and others, at least the basic conceptions of Islam,

[1] Ernst Benz, "On Understanding Non-Christian Religions," in Mircea Eliade and Joseph M. Kitagawa (eds.), *The History of Religions: Essays in Methodology* (Chicago, 1959), p. 131.

Hinduism, and Buddhism are becoming accessible to an intelligent and sympathetic Western reader.

Such progress has certainly *not* been made in the understanding of "primitive"[2] religions. Some anthropologists and historians of religions are growing increasingly aware of this situation. One has only to read the recent book by the Oxford anthropologist E. E. Evans-Pritchard, *Theories of Primitive Religion*, to understand the main reasons for the failure. Evans-Pritchard presents and criticizes some of the most popular theories of primitive religions, from E. B. Tylor to Lucien Lévy-Bruhl and Bronislaw Malinowski. The same ground had been covered, at least in part, by Robert H. Lowie in his *Primitive Religions* (1925; revised edition 1947) and *History of Ethnological Theory* (1937), by Wilhelm Schmidt in *The Origin and Growth of Religion* (1931; the original German edition was published in 1930) and by Ugo Bianchi, in *Storia della Etnologia* (1963). There is no need to summarize here these critical re-examinations of so many famous and, at one time or another, widely accepted theories. But it now seems obvious that all these hypotheses, theories, and "historical" reconstructions are more significant for the cultural history of the Western world than they are useful for the understanding of the primitive religions.

As a matter of fact, the history of ethnological theories,

---

[2] The term "primitive" is ambiguous and inconsistent; see *inter alia* Francis L. K. Hsu, "Rethinking the Concept 'Primitive,'" *Current Anthropology*, V (June, 1964), 169–78. But it entered the everyday language and it is still widely used by anthropologists. We designate by "primitive" the archaic, traditional (i.e., nonacculturated), preliterate societies. See also Stanley Diamond, "The Search for the Primitive," in *Man's Image in Medicine and Anthropology*, ed. by I. Galdston (New York, 1963), pp. 62–115.

and particularly the history of the theories of primitive religions, constitutes an ideal subject for a "history of ideas" type of monograph. We begin to realize now how much the Western consciousness has profited from the encounters with exotic and nonfamiliar cultures. I am not referring to the amount of "information" eventually acquired. I am thinking only of the creative results of such cultural encounters (for instance, Picasso and the discovery of African art, etc.). No similar "creative results" can be detected among the theories elaborated in confrontation with primitive religions. Nevertheless, these theories are part and parcel of Western cultural history. No matter how imperfect or irrelevant they may be, they disclose the modern man's profound uneasiness in approaching "primitive" people and in trying to understand "archaic" modes of being.

It is refreshing to read the verdict of an anthropologist apropos of the religious illiteracy of so many writers on primitive religions. Evans-Pritchard does not hesitate to affirm that had they "read at all deeply into, shall we say, Christian theology, history, exegesis, apologetics, symbolic thought, and ritual, they would have been much better placed to assess accounts of primitive religious ideas and practices."[3] This is certainly true, and no historian of religions will fail to underscore such statements.[4] But, on the

[3] E. E. Evans-Pritchard, *Theories of Primitive Religion* (Oxford, 1965), pp. 16–17.

[4] The same author also emphasizes the necessity of integrating the study of primitive religion into the larger perspective of history of religions. "Now, sooner or later, if we are to have a general sociological theory of religion, we shall have to take into consideration all religions and not just primitive religions; and only by so doing can we understand some of its most essential features" (*Theories of Primitive Religion*, p. 113).

other hand, religious literacy as such does not guarantee a correct understanding of primitive religions. Whichever may be the case, religious illiteracy or literacy, the Western investigator approaches the "primitive world" with certain ideological presuppositions. It is the very fact of "primitivism" that has fascinated researchers for at least the past two hundred years. A preliminary question was more or less tacitly guiding their inquiries: do the contemporary "primitives" represent, religiously speaking, a stage very near the "absolute beginning" or, on the contrary, do the primitives (or most of them) display a more or less catastrophic "degeneration," a fall from a primordial perfect situation?

We may call these two antagonistic orientations "evolutionist" and "romantic-decadentist." The first trend was more in favor with the general positivistic *Zeitgeist* of the nineteenth century. As a matter of fact, it dominated the learned world from Auguste Comte and Herbert Spencer to E. B. Tylor and Sir James Frazer. The second orientation, related both to the Enlightenment's Noble Savage ideology and to Christian theology, first received a degree of scientific prestige with Andrew Lang and Wilhelm Schmidt, but never became popular among ethnologists and historians of religions.

Notwithstanding their radical differences, these ideologies have two things in common: 1) their obsession with the *origin* and the *beginnings* of religions; 2) their taking for granted that the beginning was something "simple and pure." Of course, the evolutionists and the romantic-decadentists understood quite differently this primordial simplicity. For the evolutionists, "simple" meant *elementary*, that is, something very near animal behavior. For the romantic-decadentists, the primitive simplicity was either a form of spiritual plenitude and perfection (Lang, Schmidt) or the naive simplicity of the Noble Savage before his corruption and degeneration brought on by civilization (Rousseau, Enlightenment). Both these ideologies postulated the unfolding of archaic religions as a linear movement from the simple to the complex, though in opposite directions; up (the evolutionists) or down (the romantic-decadentists). But such interpretations implied a *naturalistic* or a *theological* approach, not a *historical* one.

Western scholarship spent almost a century in working out a number of hypothetical reconstructions of the "origin and development" of primitive religions.[5] Sooner or later all these labors became obsolete, and today they are relevant only for the history of the Western mind. For the past thirty or forty years the "historicity" of primitive cultures and religions has universally been accepted. No contemporary ethnologist or historian of religions believes that the primitives are or have been *Naturvölker*, that they neither live in nor have been changed by History. The main difference in comparison with other types of culture consists in the fact that the primitives are not so much interested in what we call "history," that is, in the series of irreversible events taking place in linear, historical time. They are concerned rather with their own "sacred history," that is, with the mythical and creative acts which founded their culture

[5] This was, of course in line with the general trend of nineteenth-century ideology; see M. Eliade, "The Quest for the 'Origins' of Religion," *History of Religions*, IV (Summer, 1964), 154–169, reprinted in *The Quest* (Chicago: University of Chicago Press, 1969), pp. 37–53.

and institutions, and bestowed meaning upon human existence.

This particular attitude of the primitives toward history
constitutes a rather intricate problem, which we cannot debate here. What interests us for the moment is the fact that
the discovery and acceptance of primitive historicity did
not have the results which would have been expected from
such a decisive change, namely the passage from a naturalistic (or theological) approach to a historical one. Indeed,
far too much time and energy have been devoted to hypothetical reconstructions of the history of different primitive religions. But even if the results of all these laborious
analyses were convincing (and this is not always the case),
the real problems raised by accepting the historicity of
primitive religions are not answered. Ultimately, what we
desire to know is the *meaning* of the various historical
modifications that took place in a given archaic religion.
We know that a historical change (for instance, the passage
from food-collecting to the sedentary stage, the borrowing
of a foreign technological invention or institution, etc.) has
also a religious meaning, since a number of symbols, myths,
and rituals emerge as a result of the process. In other words,
the modifications brought out by historical circumstances
were not passively received, but occasioned new religious
creations. We must always keep in mind the religious creativity of archaic man. The fact that so many primitives
have not only survived but prospered and developed until
direct and massive contact with the Europeans, proves their
spiritual creativity. And at that level of culture spiritual is
tantamount to *religious*. Moreover, religious creativity is independent of technological progress. The Australians, for

example, have elaborated a magnificent religious system, though their technology remained elementary.

In sum, the discovery and acceptance of the historicity of the primitives have not given rise to any adequate hermeneutics of the archaic religions. Studying a tribe as a historical continuum rather than as a *Naturvolk* marks great progress, but this is not enough. The "sacred history" of the primitives ought to be considered a work of the human mind, and not be demythologized in order to reduce it to a "projection" of psychological, sociological, or economic conditions. Reductionism as a general method for grasping certain types of "reality" may help to solve Western man's problems, but it is irrelevant as a hermeneutical tool. It is irrelevant particularly in the case of archaic cultures. For primitive man's creativity is *religious* par excellence. His ethical, institutional, and artistic creations are dependent on, or inspired by, religious experience and thought. Only if we take seriously these *oeuvres*—in the same way that we take seriously the Old Testament, the Greek tragedies, or the works of Dante, Shakespeare, and Goethe—will the primitives find their proper place in the unfolding of the universal history, in continuity with other creative peoples of past and present. It is not enough to repeat that the primitives are neither "savages" nor "prelogical" peoples, that they can think as consistently as the Westerners, and that their social structures and economic systems abundantly substantiate their theoretical maturity and their empirical alertness. This is certainly true, but it does not further our understanding. It emphatically proclaims that the primitives are "normal" human beings, but it does not show that they are also *creative*. Only a competent hermeneutical work, carried out on the ensemble of the archaic religious expressions, will be able to grasp and interpret the specific dimensions of this type of creativity.

It is to be expected that some time in the future the political and cultural representatives of the new states of Africa or Oceania, that is, the descendants of what we still call "primitives," will strongly object to the anthropological expeditions and the other varieties of field work. They will rightly point out that their peoples have too long been the "objects" of such investigations, with rather disappointing results. Indeed, as is well known, the main interest of Western scholars has been the study of material cultures and the analysis of family structure, social organization, tribal law, and so on. These are problems, one may say, important and even urgent for Western scholarship, but of secondary importance for the understanding of the *meaning of a particular culture*, as it was understood and assumed *by its own members*. (Broader, sympathetic, and intelligent studies like those of Marcel Griaule, Evans-Pritchard, Victor Turner, Ad. E. Jenson, or R. G. Lienhardt, and a few other cultural anthropologists are rather exceptional.) Those in charge of the new African states, for example, might decide rather to engage Western scholars to study and interpret their great *spiritual creations*—their religious systems, mythologies, and folklores, their plastic arts, their dances—instead of a particular and minor aspect of their society or technology. They will also demand to be judged on the basis of these *oeuvres*, and not on the basis of their family structures, social organization, or superstitions. Exactly, they might add, as French culture must be approached and judged on its masterpieces—the cathedral of Chartres, the works of Racine, Pascal, and all other great works of the mind—and not, for example, on the study of village versus urban economy, or fluctuations of the birthrate, or the rise of anticlericalism in the nineteenth century, or the growth of the yellow novel, or many other problems of the same type. The latter are certainly part of French social and cultural history, but are neither representative nor illustrative of French genius.[6]

One of the most recent misunderstandings is related precisely to the recognition of the primitive "normality." Once it was admitted that the primitives were not savage or mentally retarded but normal and healthy human beings, scholars tried to find out how close primitives were to their Western contemporaries. Of course, for some psychologists there is almost no difference between the primitives and the twentieth-century Westerners. But this truism does not help us to understand the primitives, for we still judge individuals and peoples not by their being psychologically normal, but by their creativity. Other scholars pointed out that the archaic mind was not stagnant, that some primitives made important technological discoveries (for instance, Murdock claims that agriculture was rediscovered by the Africans), that some others had a certain sense of history (for instance, their oral traditions conserve the souvenirs of important historical events), or even that certain Australian

---

[6] Besides, we must also expect a reaction against the traditional academic usage, allowing an investigator, after a longer or a shorter period of "field work," to publish a monograph on the culture or religion of that particular population. We may well imagine how the efforts of an Asian or African investigator will be received if he knows almost nothing of the history of Christianity, studies the religious life in a village of southern France for a year or two, and then writes a monograph entitled *The Religion of France.*

tribes have anticipated some of the newest mathematical theories, and so on.

All this may be true, but for our purpose it is irrelevant. One may even suspect an unconscious desire to keep the primitives somewhere *behind* us, in the neolithic period, in the middle ages, in a protocapitalist era, and so forth. It looks like an effort to situate the primitives in the perspective of a linear history, and this is *our* history. Such being the case, in spite of all the generous and enthusiastic proclamations of the basic equality between archaic and modern Western man, the final result is not encouraging for the primitives. Their technological discoveries might have been important for the neolithic, but they stopped there, and their scientific inventive genius can be compared to neither that of the Greek nor the early Chinese, to say nothing of that of the modern Western world. Neither does the possession of a certain "sense of history" suffice to approximate the primitives to the Hebrews. All this amounts to saying that the primitives were capable of some discoveries which played important roles in the rise of the West, but that for one reason or another, very few of them made significant progress along these lines. Ultimately, this means that the primitives are *behind* us, and that if in the near future they will be able to reach the Western status, it will be because they were helped to attain that goal.

I do not think that such an approach is historically correct. Whatever might have been the contribution of the primitives to the advance of science and technology, their real genius was not expressed on that level. If we take seriously their historicity, that is, their positive answers to historical changes and crisis, we should admit that their creativity was expressed almost exclusively on the religious plane. We must not judge all human spiritual works with a modern Western scale of values. This is evident even *within* the history of Western culture. The masterpieces of European literary folklore are independent of Homer, Dante, or Racine, and have almost nothing to do with their esthetic presuppositions. They are not, for this reason, less important literary masterpieces. We must accept a spiritual creation in its own frame of reference. The creativity of the primitives achieved its maximum on the religious level. This is enough to assure their place in universal history. But the condition is that we make the effort to understand correctly these religious expressions; in other words, that we elaborate what may be called a "creative hermeneutics" of the archaic religious worlds.

Australian Religions is based on a course I gave at the University of Chicago in 1964. I am grateful to my former students Nancy Auer and Alf Hiltebeitel for their care in correcting and stylistically improving the text, which was published in *History of Religions*. This preface first appeared as "On Understanding Primitive Religions," in *Glaube und Geschichte* (Festschrift für Ernst Benz), published by E. J. Brill in 1967.

Mircea Eliade

University of Chicago

AUSTRALIAN RELIGIONS

An Introduction

CHAPTER 1

Supernatural Beings
and High Gods

There is a general belief among the Australians that the world, man, and the various animals and plants were created by certain Supernatural Beings who afterward disappeared, either ascending to the sky or entering the earth. The act of "creation" was not so much a cosmogony as it was a molding and transformation of a pre-existent material; it was not a *creatio ex nihilo* but the shaping of an amorphous cosmic substance that had already existed before the appearance of the Supernatural Beings. In a similar fashion, the "creation" of man was rather a modification of a previously shapeless or monstrous being. The myths tend to emphasize the morphological completion and spiritual instruction of the primeval man rather than his coming to life from a pre-existent material form. Man was truly *made* when he received his present form and when the religious, social, and cultural institutions which were henceforth to constitute the most precious heritage of his tribe were revealed to him.

The coming into being of man and the actual world took place in the Dream Time—the *alchera* or *alcheringa* time, to use the Aranda terms for this primordial and fabulous epoch. The physical landscape was changed, and man became what he is today as the result of a series of deeds by Supernatural Beings. Nowhere in Australia do these creative acts of the "Dream Time" personages impress us with their grandeur. As a matter of fact, the majority of the central Australian "creation myths" tell only of the long and monotonous wanderings of different types of Primordial Beings; in the course of these wanderings they modified the landscape, produced plants and animals, and performed a series of "rituals" which ever since have been scrupulously repeated by the aborigines. The narratives of these creative acts constitute what we call "myths"; indeed, they are "sacred" and serve as foundations and justifications for the entire religious life of the tribe. The "Dream Time" came to an end when the Supernatural Beings left the surface of the earth. But the mythical past was not lost forever; on the contrary, it is periodically recovered through the tribal rituals. As we shall see, the most sacred and especially the secret ceremonies are supposed to reactualize the mythical events, thus rendering present the fabulous time of the beginnings.

As is the case with all other "primitive" religions, to understand the Australian religion ultimately means to know what happened *in illo tempore*, that is to say, what type of Primordial Beings made their appearance at the very beginning, what kind of activity they carried out—and to what purpose—and what became of them afterward. As is to be expected, the most animated debate between scholars has been the one concerned with the type or structure of the Primordial Beings: were they Sky Gods, "All-Fathers"; theriomorphic mythical ancestors; ghosts of famous chieftains? This controversy is extremely significant both for the comprehension of Australian religions and for the history of the understanding of archaic religions by Western scholars—in fact, the debate is revealing for the history of the modern Western mind in general.

For this reason we shall dwell in some detail on the discussion concerning a specific class of Australian Primordial Beings, the so-called All-Fathers or Sky Beings of the southeastern tribes. As these populations have disappeared or have been too rapidly civilized, we do not possess their complete mythologies. But enough information has been gathered by observers during the second half of the nineteenth century, and particularly by A. W. Howitt, to enable us to grasp the structure of their religions. The main characteristic of all these populations is their belief in supernatural Sky Beings. To simplify this presentation, I will use almost exclusively the data of Howitt. But references to some of the earlier authorities will be made later on, when we will discuss the impact of Howitt's observations on contemporary scholarship.

The Sky Beings of Southeast Australia

In his book on the Narrinyeri tribe, published in 1847, George Taplin wrote that these aborigines "call the Supreme Being by the names *Nurrundere* and *Martummere*. He is said to have made all things on the earth, and to have given to men the weapons of war and hunting, and to have instituted all the rites and ceremonies which are practised by the aborigines, whether connected with life or death. On inquiring why they adhere to any custom, the reply is: *Nurrundere* commanded it. *Nurrundere* went to Wyrra-warre, taking his children with him."[1] Wyrra-warre is said

---

[1] George Taplin, *The Narrinyeri: An Account of the Tribe of Australian Aborigines Inhabiting the Country around the Lakes Alexandrina, Albert, and Coorong* (Adelaide, 1847), p. 55; quoted by A. W. Howitt, *The Native Tribes of South-East Australia* (hereinafter cited as "*Native Tribes*") (London: Macmillan, 1904), p. 488. A critical examination of Taplin's data is found in Wilhelm

to be the sky, and Taplin adds that "the Narrinyeri always mention his name with reverence." He relates that during a great kangaroo hunt, "on reaching the hunting-ground, a wallaby, which had been killed on the road thither, was produced, and a fire kindled by the women. Then the men standing round, struck up a sort of chant, at the same time stamping with their feet. The wallaby was put on the fire, and as the smoke from it ascended, the hunters, at a concerted signal, rushed towards it, lifting their weapons towards heaven. I afterwards learned that this ceremony was instituted by *Nurrundere*."[2] This scene recalled to Howitt the commencement of a certain ritual, when the men pointed to the sky with their weapons or with branches, "as indicating the great Biambun, whose name is not lawful to mention excepting at the ceremonies, and only when initiated persons are present."[3]

Another tribe, the Wiimbaio, believes that Nurelli made the whole country, together with its trees and animals. After giving laws to the aborigines he went up to the sky, and he is now one of the constellations.[4] According to the myths of Wotjobaluk, Bunjil, the Supreme Being, once lived on the earth as a Great Man but eventually ascended to the sky. Bunjil is also called "Our Father."[5] Other Supreme Beings of the southeastern tribes—Baiame, Daramulun, Mungan-ngaua—likewise are spoken of as "fathers."

Schmidt, *Ursprung der Gottesidee* (hereinafter cited as *"Ursprung"*), I (2d ed.; Münster, 1926), 328, 399 ff., 408.

[2] Taplin, *The Narrinyeri*, p. 55; quoted by A. W. Howitt, *Native Tribes*, pp. 488–89.

[3] Howitt, *Native Tribes*, p. 489.

[4] *Ibid.*

[5] *Ibid.*, pp. 489–90.

Mungan-ngaua, for example, literally means "Father of All of Us."[6] The Kulin and the Wurungerri describe Bunjil as an old man with two wives; his son is Binbeal, the rainbow. Bunjil taught the Kulin the arts of life and social institutions. Then he ascended to the sky land; from there he supervises the tribe. Howitt points out that this celestial being was usually referred to as Mami-ngata, that is, "Our Father," rather than by his name Bunjil. Howitt was also impressed with the fact that the human element predominates over the animal in these myths.[7]

It is important to note that knowledge of the names and myths of these Supreme Beings of the southeastern tribes is restricted to the initiates. Women and children know almost nothing about them. Among the Kurnai, for example, the women know only that there is a Supreme Being in the sky called Mungan-ngaua, "Father of All of Us."[8] In fact, it is only during the final and most secret stage of the initiation that the novice learns the most essential myth—namely, that Mungan-ngaua lived on the earth a long time ago and taught the ancestors of the Kurnai all the elements of their culture. Mungan-ngaua founded the secret rites of the initiation (jeraeil), and his married son, Tundum, conducted them for the first time, using the two bull-roarers that bear the names of him and his wife. But a traitor revealed the mysteries of the jeraeil to the women. In his anger Mungan-

---

[6] Ibid., pp. 490–91.

[7] Ibid., p. 492.

[8] Howitt once met an old woman, a survivor of the Theddora tribe, and when he asked her about Daramulun she answered: "All that I know of Daramulun is that he comes down with a noise like thunder, to make the boys into men. We call him Papang" (ibid., p. 493). Papang, Howitt explains, means "Father." The "noise like thunder" is that of the bull-roarers.

ngaua brought on a cosmic cataclysm in which almost the entire human race perished; soon afterward he ascended into the sky. His son Tundum and Tundum's wife were both turned into porpoises.[9]

There is obviously a great difference between what was known *before* the initiation—the fact that there is a celestial "Father" whose voice resembles that of the distant thunder —and what the neophyte discovers in the course of the secret rites. He learns the myth of the Supreme Being: his creative deeds, his anger, and his disappearance from the earth. He also learns that the disappearance of Mungan-ngaua brought to an end a fabulous period. In sum, the neophyte discovers that a series of dramatic and sometimes catastrophic events took place in a mythical past. As we shall see, the revelation of the secret and traditional "sacred stories" constitutes the core of every Australian initiation ceremony, even among those tribes that do not share the belief in a celestial Supreme Being.

To help complete the picture afforded by our scanty data of the southeastern tribes, we might add a few more examples. According to the Kamilaroi, Baiame created all things. Though generally invisible, Baiame has appeared in human form, bestowing various gifts on the tribe.[10] During his initiation the Yuin novice learns the myth of Daramulun ("Father"; he is also called Biamban, "Master"). Long ago, Daramulun dwelt on earth with his mother. The earth was barren, hard, and sterile as a stone—and there were no

[9] *Ibid.*, p. 630. See also M. Eliade, *Birth and Rebirth* (New York: Harper, 1958), pp. 10–31 (reprinted as *Rites and Symbols of Initiation* [New York: Harper Torchbooks]); subsequent references are to the 1958 edition.

[10] Howitt, *Native Tribes*, p. 494.

human beings, only animals. Daramulun created the ancestor of the Yuin and taught him how to live. He gave him the laws which are handed down from father to son, founded the initiation ceremonies, and made the bull-roarer, the sound of which represents his voice. It is Daramulun who gives the medicine men their powers. And when a man dies, Daramulun meets and cares for his spirit.[11]

As Howitt has already pointed out, all of these names—Bunjil, Baiame, Daramulun, and so forth—most probably refer to the same divinity. "He is evidently everlasting, for he existed from the beginnings of all things, and he still lives."[12] There is no doubt that the belief in such a celestial Supreme Being belongs among the most archaic and genuine traditions of the southeastern aborigines. The belief was witnessed before the installation of the Christian missions. Furthermore, as we have noted, the names, the myths, and the rituals associated with the High Beings are most secret, being revealed exclusively to the initiates. If the Supreme Being should be suspected of being merely a result of missionary propaganda, one must wonder why he is unknown to the women and why he became so central to those religious and social traditions that belong to the mythical past.[13] We might add that the same type of divinity, considered to have created the world and man and to have ascended to heaven after bestowing upon man the rudiments of culture, is attested in many other archaic religions. It is difficult for us to imagine that missionary propaganda

[11] *Ibid.*, p. 495.

[12] *Ibid.*, p. 500.

[13] *Ibid.*, pp. 501 ff. Schmidt examined the value of Howitt's personal observations at great length and criticized some of his conclusions; see *Ursprung*, I, 211–47, 296–301, etc.; see also Vol. III (Münster, 1931), Index, *s.v.*

would have given rise everywhere to the same type of
divinity and to the same mythological pattern.

The Story of a Controversy

When Howitt published his book in 1904, most of the
facts concerning the Supreme Beings of southeast Australia
were already known from his own articles in the *Journal of
the Anthropological Institute* (*JAI*), 1882–87,[14] and also
from the information brought together by Andrew Lang
in his work *The Making of Religion* (London, 1889). One
may suspect that, without the intervention of Lang, the
facts communicated by Howitt would have played a more
important role in the interpretation of Australian religion.
As a matter of fact, in the 1904 monograph Howitt watered
down his first evaluation of the High Gods, as presented in
the articles of the *JAI*. One reason for this change of mind
might have been the tumult raised by Lang's book. It is true
that E. B. Tylor, in his article "Limits of Savage Religion"
(*JAI*, XXI [1891], 283–301), had tried to explain the Australian High Gods in terms of the direct or indirect influence of Christian missionaries. Nonetheless, this hypothesis
was not very convincing, although in some instances a
Christian influence was plausible.[15] But in pleading for the

---

[14] See, e.g., the following articles by A. W. Howitt in the *JAI*:
"On Some Australian Beliefs" (XIII [1884], 185–98); "The Jeraeil,
or Initiation Ceremonies of the Kurnai Tribe" (XIV [1885],
301–27); "On the Migration of the Kurnai Ancestors" (XV
[1886], 409–27); and "On Australian Medicine Men" (XVI [1887],
23–58).

[15] Howitt knew from his long and intensive work among the
southeastern Australian tribes that Tylor's theory was untenable.
See also N. W. Thomas, "Baiame and the Bell-Bird," *Man* (1905),
pp. 44–52; Schmidt, *Ursprung*, I, 249 ff.

authenticity of the Australian beliefs Lang had made the mistake, astutely pointed out by E. S. Hartland,[16] of presenting the Australian gods almost in Christian terms. Hartland rightly remarked that the Australians do not speak of "immortality" or "eternity" but of "very long life." (What Hartland did not realize was that these plastic expressions, "long life," "old age," and so on, fill the same function as the "immortality" or "eternity" of the other, more elaborate religions.)

Another methodological error was Lang's tendency to consider the mythical element as secondary or aberrant. Lang labeled as "myths"—which for him were "obscene or humorous tales"—everything he did not like in a "primitive" religion; we shall dwell upon this ideological prejudice later on. He was nevertheless impressed by Hartland's criticism, and in his reply he reminded his opponent that already in his *Myth, Ritual and Religion* (Vol. I [London, 1901], chap. xi) he had admitted the coexistence of "the *mythical* and the *religious* elements in beliefs."[17] But Hartland rightly emphasized that this implies an acknowledgment of the justice of his criticism.[18]

---

[16] See E. S. Hartland, "The 'High Gods' of Australia," *Folk-lore*, IX (1898), 290–329.

[17] Andrew Lang, "Australian Gods: A Reply," *Folk-lore*, X (1899), 1–46; see p. 14.

[18] E. S. Hartland, "Australian Gods: Rejoinder," *Folk-lore*, X (1899), 46–57; see p. 50. The Lang-Hartland controversy was laboriously analyzed by Schmidt in *Ursprung* (I, 273–311) in the enormous chapter "Die Kritik der Theorie Langs" (pp. 211–487), which follows the chapter devoted to "Der monotheistic Präanimismus A. Langs" (pp. 134–210). Another discussion of Lang's ideas is to be found in Raffaelle Pettazzoni, *Dio: Formazione e sviluppo del monoteismo nella storia delle religioni* (Rome, 1922), I, 43–50. See below, n. 33.

Lang continued to fight for the recognition of Howitt's discoveries; he even fought against Howitt's own interpretation of his discoveries. In an article entitled "God (Primitive and Savage),"[19] Lang once again summarized his arguments in favor of the authenticity of the Australian All-Fathers, first quoting the following letter written by Baldwin Spencer to J. G. Frazer on August 19, 1902:

As to the "discovery" of a high ethical religion amongst the lowest savages there is not, I am convinced, any such thing in Australia. The great difficulty is that we have had statements made on the authority of men like Gason. The latter was a police-trooper, I believe, who was perfectly honest, but at the same time perfectly incapable of dealing with matters such as these. In the days when the evidence of Baiame and Daramulun was collected the importance of securing minute and detailed information was really not realized, nor was it imagined that there were men without any so-called religious ideas; and as I have endeavoured to point out in one of our chapters, it is the easiest thing possible to be misled by what a native tells you in regard to such a point as this.[20]

But Lang sarcastically remarks ("God [Primitive and Savage]," p. 244a), "Spencer must have forgotten that the chief authority on Daramulun is Howitt' (cf. *Native Tribes*, pp. 494 ff., 526, 528, 543). Lang was by now well aware of the fact that most of the oldest authors were suspected either of an imperfect scientific training or of a religious bias. Thus he acknowledges that James Manning, although

[19] Andrew Lang, "God (Primitive and Savage)," in J. Hastings (ed.), *Encyclopaedia of Religion and Ethics*, VI (Edinburgh, 1913), 243–47. In this article Lang uses many examples already quoted in his discussion with Hartland.

[20] J. G. Frazer, *Totemism and Exogamy*, I (London, 1910), 148.

"he began his researches about 1833–34, when missionaries had not arrived, Melbourne did not exist and there were no churches near his station," erred in representing Baiame and Grogorally too closely "to the Father and Son of Christian doctrine." But he points out that Manning's account was corroborated by Mrs. Langloh Parker, in her book *The Euahlayi Tribe* (London, 1905). And he stresses the fact that a benevolent and creative being was attested "in 1833, 1855 and 1889–95 by three witnesses, all very intimate with the Kamilaroi and Euahlayi tribes," and that their information precedes by many years the appearance of missionaries.[21]

Likewise, Lang shows that A. L. P. Cameron, our chief informant on the "nations" of Itchumundi, Karamundi, and Barkingi and the author of a long description of the All-Father of these tribes,[22] cannot be easily dismissed; indeed, he was accepted by Frazer as an authority for the totemic institutions of these tribes (cf. *Totemism and Exogamy*, I, 380–87). Again, Lang reproaches Frazer (p. 151) for quoting the opinion expressed by E. M. Curr in *The Australian Race* (I [London, 1886–87], 45) that the aborigines dress up what they have learned from missionaries "with a view to please and surprise the whites," without informing his readers that Howitt (*Native Tribes*, pp. 503–6) had "replied and crushed Curr." Indeed, Howitt had shown that the Kurnai were not exposed to missionary propaganda. To

[21] On Manning and Mrs. Parker, see also Lang, "Australian Gods," pp. 26 ff., 28 ff. A fresh analysis of their information was undertaken by Schmidt, *Ursprung*, I, 151–52 (Manning), 304 ff., 358 ff. (Mrs. Parker).

[22] A. L. P. Cameron, "Notes on Some Tribes of New South Wales," *JAI*, XIV (1885), 351 ff.

the contrary, Lang continues, "where missions have long
settled, as among the Dieiri and the Southern Arunta, not
the farthest ray of Gospel light was discovered by Spencer
and Gillen among the Arunta, or by Howitt or his informants among the Dieiri. Howitt found only a daemon
named Brewin among the Kurnai (see *Kamilaroi and
Kurnai* [Melbourne, 1881]) till he was initiated into their
esoteric rites and doctrines."[23]

Finally, Lang discusses Howitt's own ideas concerning
the All-Fathers. He reminds us that in 1881, while still uninitiated, Howitt knew nothing of this belief.

In 1884–85 he wrote copiously and with some enthusiasm
about it in the *Journal of the Anthropological Institute*. He
then spoke of the being as "the Supreme Spirit, who appears to
me to represent the defunct headman." In 1904 Howitt [*Native
Tribes*, p. 503] renounced the idea that the All-Father is a
spirit, but still regarded him as an idealization of a tribal "headman," who had created the world or most of it, among other
wonderful works, and whose very name was tabued among
men on earth except on the most sacred occasions. He "can go
anywhere and do anything." In the same work Howitt rather
watered down his expressions of 1884–85 [Lang, "God (Primitive and Savage)," p. 245a].

Howitt was convinced that the belief in the All-Fathers
"was a concomitant of social advance on the coast and in
well-watered countries." But Lang reminds Howitt that
"he had recorded the belief among tribes with the simplest
and most archaic social organization . . . and among tribes
as far removed from the sea and in conditions as unfavor-
able as the peoples of the Darling River and its hinter-
land" (*ibid.*). And Spencer and F. J. Gillen had discovered

[23] Lang, "God (Primitive and Savage)," p. 245a.

the High Being Atnatu among the Kaitish tribe, in the arid and infertile center of Australia. On the contrary, no All-Father belief was identified by Spencer and Gillen among the Aranda, with their highly advanced social organization (but see below, pp. 28 ff.).

Andrew Lang quotes the lines in which Howitt admits that the All-Father "is evidently everlasting, for he existed from the beginning of all things, and he still lives. But in being so, he is merely in that state in which, these aborigines believe, everyone would be if not prematurely killed by magic" (*Native Tribes*, p. 503). But, Lang comments, only men can be killed, and not the All-Father, who existed before death entered the world. "In this being," continues Howitt, "although supernatural, there is no trace of a divine nature" (*ibid.*)—words that surprise Lang: No trace of a divine nature, he exclaims, "in a benevolent and everlasting creator, in several cases the dispenser of reward and penalty in the future life!" Howitt concludes that "it cannot be alleged that these aborigines have consciously any form of religion," because no sacrifice is offered and (except in very rare cases) no prayer is addressed to the All-Father. And again Lang ironically reminds Howitt that he himself had discovered and described the worship of Daramulun.[24]

From "Men without Religion" to *Urmonotheismus*

This controversy on the nature and structure of the Australian High Gods was entangled in a series of preju-

---

[24] In the last section of this article (*ibid.*) Lang discusses the beliefs of the Aranda and Dieiri tribes, and especially their *alcheringa* heroes and *mura-mura*, who live in the sky and are called upon by the Dieiri for rain; for Lang this is a form of religion, because it implies prayers to a supernatural power.

dices. The "evolutionist" scholars (Spencer, Frazer, Hartland, and others) were convinced of the impossibility of a
genuinely high religious conception among the Australian
aborigines, for they were convinced of the aborigines' mental and spiritual inferiority. They found it impossible to
believe that a "stone-age" man was capable of elaborating
such a complex and "noble" figure as that of a Creator, an
omniscient and ethical All-Father. This type of divine
figure was expected only at the apex of the religious evolution, not at an early stage. As Hartland puts it: "As little
. . . as the Australian theology do the precepts taught in
the Australian mysteries, when carefully examined, yield
evidence of anything higher than the state of savagery in
which the natives are found."[25] Moreover, there was also,
at least unconsciously, an implicit conviction of the religious, or "scientific," justification for the white man's
conquest of the black fellow's continent.

But similar, if not so gross, prejudices were at work
among the other party. Lang and his enthusiastic follower,
Pater Wilhelm Schmidt, were equally "rationalists," though
of another type. Lang thought that mythical creativity was
somehow a sign of degeneration. Because he had discovered
very few myths associated with the Australian All-Fathers,
he thought that myth was secondary and ultimately disruptive of the highly ethical religious values. "Among the lowest known tribes we usually find, just as in Ancient Greece,
the belief in a deathless 'Father,' 'Master,' 'Maker,' and also
the crowd of humorous, obscene, fanciful myths which are
in flagrant contradiction with the religious character of that
belief. That belief is what we call rational, and even ele-

[25] "The 'High Gods' of Australia," p. 328.

vated. The myths, on the other hand, are what we call irrational and debasing." And he adds: "The religious conception uprises from the human intellect, in one mood, that of earnest contemplation and submission; while the mythical ideas uprise from another mood, that of playful and erratic fancy."[26]

Now it is a characteristically and inveterately Western and rationalistic approach to separate "myth" from "religion" and to proclaim that this separation of "irrational" from "rational" elements can be justified by historical research: "in the beginning" archaic man disposed of a very simple, rational, and ethical "religion"; then the "playful and erratic fancy" intervened and spoiled everything. But fortunately a "good religion" can always reverse the process and purify itself by *Entmythologisierung*. As a matter of fact, the myth is the ground of religion. And nowhere else is this situation more clearly illustrated than in Australia: we always find the myth *at the beginning* of religion—of any type of religion. It is true that the "All-Fathers" or Sky Beings have fewer myths than other Supernatural Beings, but this fact—which is attested throughout the entire history of religion—has another explanation than the "secondary character" of myth postulated by Lang.

While Lang was writing his last article on the High Gods, Wilhelm Schmidt was completing the first volume of his monumental *Ursprung der Gottesidee*.[27] By that time

[26] Lang, *Myth, Ritual and Religion*, I (London, 1901), 4–5.

[27] The work first appeared in French, between 1908 and 1910, in *Anthropos*, the new journal founded by Schmidt. The reprint also was circulated separately under the title *L'Origine de l'idée de Dieu. Etude historico-critique et positive. Première partie: Historico-critique* (Vienna, 1910). The German text was published in 1912, and a second, enlarged, edition appeared in 1926.

he had already acquired the prestige of a great linguist and ethnologist, and he had published an imposing number of books and monographs. He spared no pains in reading, analyzing, criticizing, and interpreting all the available materials on the Australian High Gods, with a view toward substantiating, correcting, and systematizing the ideas of Lang. He thought that he would be able to explain certain contradictions in the data—and particularly the coexistence of "mythical" or "degraded" elements with the more elevated conceptions of the High Gods—in terms of various crosses between the High God beliefs and later religious creations. He applied the method of historical ethnology that had been elaborated by Fritz Graebner for the purpose of identifying different cultural and religious strata. A few years later Schmidt published in the third volume of *Ursprung der Gottesidee* a systematic presentation of the religious beliefs and customs of the southeastern Australians, covering almost six hundred pages.[28]

In his old age Schmidt complained that almost no one had read this exhaustive monograph and that very few scholars had made use of his meticulous analysis and elaborate system of cultural stratification. This is true. And, unfortunately, it is true not only with regard to the first and third volumes of *Ursprung der Gottesidee* but also the other nine volumes. (The twelfth and last volume was published posthumously in 1955.) The neglect of such a monument of learning—twelve thousand pages consecrated to

----

[28] *Ursprung*, III, the Australian materials, pp. 565–1114. Schmidt once again examines the southeastern Australian religious beliefs in Vol. VI of his *Ursprung*, entitled *Endsynthese der Religionen der Urvölker Amerikas, Asiens, Australiens, Afrikas* (Münster, 1935); see *s.v.* "Australier."

the idea of God among the most archaic peoples!—is due to many causes, some of them decidedly unworthy of the work. (A great many ethnologists and historians of religion found it impossible to believe that a Roman Catholic priest would be able to write "objectively" about primitive religion;[29] others simply refused to read so many thousands of pages by the same author; others did not read German). But there are also more serious factors that help to explain the negligible impact of *Ursprung der Gottesidee* on contemporary scholarship. One is the author's rigid and excessive rationalism, his conviction not only that an *Urmonotheismus* existed but that he could prove its existence with the help of historical ethnology. Even more than Lang, Schmidt had attempted to identify Western conceptions of divinity among the "primitives." What he called *Urmonotheismus* was not merely the belief of the most archaic populations in One creative, omniscient, and omnipotent God; it was also an awareness of the *idea* of a Supreme Being, without myths and devoid of any anthropomorphic traits and weaknesses. Pater Schmidt asserted that the idea of the Supreme Being belongs to a religious stage preceding any mythological formulation.[30] But such an assumption is in contradiction to everything that we know of *homo religiosus* in general and of primitive man in particular. A Supreme Being is always a *primordial* and *creative* Being,

[29] Against this view, see the critical—but sympathetic—appraisal of Schmidt's work by Robert H. Lowie, *The History of Ethnological Theory* (New York, 1937), pp. 77 ff.; *idem, Primitive Religion* (New York, 1924), pp. 127–31, 167–69.

[30] Already in his lecture "Die Mythologie der austronesischen Völker," *Mittheilungen der anthropologische Gesellschaft in Wien,* XXXIX (1909), 240–59; see p. 258. But Schmidt repeated this view time and time again in his writings.

and "primordiality" and "creativity" are mythical thought structures par excellence. If, almost everywhere in the world, the mythologies of the Supreme Beings are not as rich as the mythologies of the other species of divine figures, it is not because such Supreme Beings belong to a premythological epoch but simply because their activity is somehow exhausted in the works that they do *in the beginning*. They are said to have created or shaped the world and man, to have founded the principal social institutions, and to have proclaimed the moral laws. Now, the story of this type of creation is rather simple and may appear monotonous in comparison with the more dramatic mythologies of other divine beings whose works and adventures took place *after* the cosmogonic period had come to an end (although, of course, these latter works and adventures were also represented as having taken place in the primordial, mythical time).

To give only one example: the fact that Bunjil, the Supreme Being of the Kulin, is represented in his myths as having a brother, sons, daughters, and one or sometimes even two wives constitutes, for Schmidt, evidence that we are not in this instance being confronted with the original Bunjil; we are dealing with the result of a series of cross-fertilizations from later cultural strata, each of them associated with a different type of mythology. According to Schmidt, Bunjil's brother reflects the influence of the lunar mythology characteristic of the *Zweiklassenkulturen;* his wives and children are the result of the crossing of lunar and solar mythologies characteristic of the *Mischkulturen.*[31]

What is implied here is, of course, the assumption that

---

[31] See *Ursprung*, I, 342 ff., 371 ff.; III, 674–75; etc.

contact with "mythological thinking" (i.e., the lunar and solar mythologies) and with alien social structures (e.g., the *Zweiklassenkultur*) inevitably must produce a deterioration in the original representation of the Supreme Being. But the very notion of the deterioration of a noble and spiritual Figure because of his implication in "human" contradictions and behavior is an "enlightened" Western idea. In a great many archaic and traditional cultures ("primitive" cultures, the ancient Near East, India, etc.) "human" extravagances do not discredit the transcendental prestige of a deity. Furthermore, Schmidt's analysis of Bunjil's various "strata" is only a hypothetical reconstruction; it is not the description of a historical process; and it is certainly not the kind of hermeneutical work expected from a historian of religion. The historian of religion would have been expected to provide not only a hypothetical reconstruction of Bunjil (the passage from the "pure" Supreme Being to the Bunjil with the brother, wives, and children) but an interpretation of these religious changes—provided, of course, that such changes could be substantiated. The "anthropomorphic figuration" of a High Being does not necessarily imply the degeneration of an antecedent and elevated figure. It rather represents a modification of the means of expression, a new "incarnation" of a religious idea. Similarly, a theriomorphic divinity is not necessarily an inferior or a poorer religious form than an anthropomorphic one. Animals lost their numinous aura only late in the history of religions. For hundreds of thousands of years the animal forms were the expression par excellence of transcendent and sacral powers. In sum, Schmidt was correct in trying to uncover and explain the historical changes in Australian religion; but his negative appraisal of these changes was an extrapolation, the product of his Western presuppositions.

Australian High Gods and the Western Zeitgeist

But whatever might have been the limitations of Lang, Schmidt, and their respective followers, at least they have the merit of having studied an important aspect of primitive religions in general and of Australian religions in particular. The conception of a High Being—no matter how different this High Being might have been from the Supreme Beings attested in other, more complex cultures—was at least something which a great number of religions could be said to have in common. The distance between "primitives" and "civilized" man did not appear as an unbridgeable gap. But very soon after the publication of Lang's last article and the first volume of *Ursprung der Gottesidee*, the Western *Zeitgeist* changed, and the interest in the problem of High Gods faded out. Emile Durkheim's *Les Formes élémentaires de la vie religieuse* (1912), Sigmund Freud's *Totem und Tabu* (1913), Lucien Lévy-Bruhl's *Les Fonctions mentales dans les sociétés inférieures* (1910) reoriented the attention of sociologists, psychologists, historians of religion, and cultivated readers toward totemism—particularly Australian totemism—and toward what Lévy-Bruhl called *la mentalité prélogique*. We need not enter into an elaborate discussion of their respective theses and hypotheses here.[32] What is sig-

[32] See M. Eliade, "The History of Religions in Retrospect: 1912–1962," *Journal of Bible and Religion*, XXX (1963), 98–109, esp. 99 ff. reprinted in *The Quest* (Chicago, 1969), pp. 12–36, esp. 15 ff. For Emile Durkheim, the Australian High Gods are dependent upon the system of totemic beliefs. Baiame, Daramulun, Bunjil, and others seem to have been phratry totems that have been deified.

nificant for our present discussion is the fact that, even though ethnologists have repeatedly criticized and rejected these hypotheses, the *Zeitgeist* of the post-World War I period seized upon Australian totemism as a central problem, significant not only for the origin of religion but for the origins of society and culture—and even of Western man's neuroses.

The few but important works published after 1920 in which the Australian High Gods were competently discussed passed almost unnoticed. We have seen the fate of the first volumes of Schmidt's *Ursprung der Gottesidee*. In 1922, Raffaele Pettazzoni brought out the first volume of his *Dio: Formazione e sviluppo del monoteismo nella storia delle religioni*, subtitled *L'Essere celeste nelle credenze dei*

According to Durkheim, this apotheosis took place through the initiation ceremonies; see *The Elementary Forms of the Religious Life*, trans. Joseph Ward Swain (1915; reprint, New York: Collier Books, 1961), p. 329 ff. One must distinguish between Durkheim's pertinent analyses of certain aspects of Australian and other archaic religions, which are extremely valuable, and his general theory of the social origin of religion. This theory has been criticized and rejected by a majority of scholars. But the popular success of Durkheim's chef d'œuvre is due primarily to his identification of religious experience with collective enthusiasm. This means, ultimately, that *The Elementary Forms* is more important for our understanding of Western mentality than for our appraisal of primitive religion. Durkheim's popularity foretold what was to break out in most Western societies within the next ten to fifteen years. As a matter of fact, *The Elementary Forms* prepared the Western reader to understand the forthcoming events of the first European war, the rise of nationalism, and the appearance of fascism and communism. In an individualistic and agnostic anticlerical France, Durkheim emphasized the religious nature of collective interests and enthusiasm. He prepared his readers to understand how the state, the social class, or the nation can become tremendous hierophanies.

popoli primitivi. He devoted a short but substantial chapter to the Australian High Gods and also discussed at length the ideas of Lang, Howitt, Schmidt, A. van Gennep, and other scholars. Pettazzoni, who had read Vico and who recognized the significance of mythical thought, rejected almost all of the previous interpretations.[33] He did not doubt the authenticity of the Australian High Gods—not only because he had read all the important primary sources but also because he understood the figure of the High God as a product of mythical imagination. For Pettazzoni, the Australian (and other archaic) Supreme Beings are celestial gods; but ultimately they are mythical personifications of the sky and of the atmospheric phenomena (thunder, rain, rainbow, etc.). Other scholars,[34] and even Schmidt, had described some of the Australian Supreme Beings as celestial gods.[35] But Pettazzoni insisted that a Sky Being has a naturistic structure mythically perceived: he not only lives *in* the sky but his activity *is* the activity of the sky.[36]

[33] See Pettazzoni, *op. cit.*, I, 43 ff. (Lang, Schmidt), 60 ff. (a critical discussion of A. van Gennep's *Mythes et légendes d'Australie* [Paris, 1906]). Van Gennep thought that the Australian high gods are naturistic deities or, more precisely, thunder gods (*dieux-tonnerre*); see *ibid.*, Introduction, p. cxvi.

[34] E.g., Frobenius, *Im Zeitalter des Sonnesgottes* (Berlin, 1904), I, 73 ff., on Baiame; W. Foy; Th. Preuss; Graebner; etc. (see Pettazzoni, *op. cit.*, I, 64 ff.).

[35] But Schmidt denied that this implies a personification of the sky; see below, n. 37.

[36] See Pettazzoni, *op. cit.*, I, 67 ff., 355 ff., etc. Pettazzoni never published his projected second and third volumes of *Dio*, to be devoted to the "Supreme God in the Polytheistic Religions" and to the "Unique God in the Monotheistic Religions" (I, p. xvi). But in 1955 he brought out an imposing monograph, *L'Onniscienza di Dio* (Torino); on Australian High Gods, see pp. 507–12.

As was to be expected, Schmidt criticized this interpretation sharply and repeatedly.[37] His main objection was that the High God, being conceived as a *person*, could neither be derived from nor identified with the sky. The discussion between the two scholars went on for the rest of their lives.[38] In one of his last articles, Pettazzoni recognized that he was "now in partial agreement with Fr. Wilhelm Schmidt as to the non-reducibility of the Supreme Being to the Celestial Being." Nonetheless, he adds that he is still of the opinion that the Supreme Being "is not mainly the product of logico-causal thought, as Schmidt holds, but rather that this notion is the product of mythical thought."[39] But it is only necessary for us to read Pettazzoni's most recent works to see that he outgrew the main thesis of *L'Essere celeste*, namely, that the primitive Supreme Beings are "personifications" of the sky.

Pettazzoni's ideas were known and discussed only among a limited number of scholars. Probably a larger audience was acquainted with Graebner's last book, *Das Weltbild der Primitiven*, where the founder of historical ethnology summarizes his views on the Australian All-Father. About this "great creative God," Graebner writes:

[37] See, e.g., Schmidt's *Ursprung*, I, 270–73, 674–70; *Anthropos*, XXI (1926), 269–72; and *The Origin and Growth of Religion*, trans. H. J. Rose (New York, 1931), pp. 209–14.

[38] See, e.g., R. Pettazzoni, "Monoteismo e 'Urmonoteismo'" (*Studi e materiali di storia delle religioni*, XIX–XX [1943–46], 170–77) and "Das Ende des Urmonotheismus?" (*Numen*, III [1956], 1956–59; *Numen*, V [1958], 161–63).

[39] R. Pettazzoni, "The Supreme Being: Phenomenological Structure and Historical Development," in M. Eliade and J. M. Kitagawa (eds.), *The History of Religions: Essays in Methodology* (Chicago, 1959), p. 60.

Generally there exists beside him another figure, powerful but subordinate, most frequently considered to be his son, but often as the primeval ancestor of mankind. Sometimes, for instance among the Kurnai, the great god has no wife, or only an invisible one; occasionally he has produced his son without having a consort. His principal attribute is that of creator, or first cause of, at least, everything which is important for men; he is the first maker of the most important implements, as the boomerang; he is a magician whose power knows no bounds; he is the celestial chief. Knowledge of him is imparted to the youths at their initiation, when they are received into the status of men; it is given them by the elders. . . . It is moreover very important that the great god is considered not only as creator and maker of all things, but also as guardian of the tribal morality. It is of him that the legend is told how in the old days, when men had forgotten their good habits, he sent the conflagration and the flood to punish them. . . . As regards the nature and meaning of the great god, it must first be said that his existence completely satisfies the lively desire of the natives to know the cause of things. But Preuss is perhaps right in doubting that so abstract an idea as the first cause could have been capable, among primitive men, of producing a figure which is always so full of life. The god is of course also supposed to be the originator of the rites and magical practices by which man rules nature; and to this extent his existence ensures the continuance of the human race even now. . . . His pre-eminent significance and the vividness with which he has been developed are due, in this ancient culture, to another factor still, I mean the ethics. This god is the preserver, not only of the psychical, but above all of the social existence of man, and thus of his very essence."[40]

[40] F. Graebner, *Das Weltbild der Primitiven* (Munich, 1924), pp. 25–27, quoted by Schmidt, *The Origin and Growth of Religion*, pp. 247–48. Graebner published a series of articles, "Zur

High Gods and Culture Heroes

Graebner's account may be considered the last authoritative and positive account of the southeast Australian High Gods. By the beginning of this century, these tribes had lost their cultural autonomy, or even disappeared physically, and new research became almost impossible. On the other hand, the new generation of ethnologists has tended to regard the observations of earlier writers with some suspicion. For example, in their great synthetical work *The World of the First Australians*, Ronald and Catherine Berndt seem to doubt even Howitt, who "went so far as to speak of an 'All Father.' "[41] The fact that in "most of southern Australia today it is no longer possible to check on such material" (p. 202) has obliged the Berndts to let the religious beliefs of these populations pass almost unnoticed. In 1943, at Menindee, they were unable to obtain an articulate Baiame myth. "He was still well known, but allusions to him were mainly in the context of initation and magic, and to his appearance during certain rites" (*ibid.*). Even in an acculturated society, the secret cult of a High Being would seem to be the most resistant![42]

---

australischen Religionsgeschichte," in *Globus*, 96 (1909), 341 ff., 362 ff., 373 ff., in which he attempted to establish the chronology of the three distinct cultural areas that he had previously discovered. Graebner's research and his results, for obvious reasons, were ignored by Durkheim. See also Rudolph F. Lehmann, "Die Religionen Australiens und der Südsee, 1911–1930," *Archiv für Religionswissenschaft*, XXIX (1931), 139–86.

[41] R. M. and C. H. Berndt, *The World of the First Australians* (Chicago: University of Chicago Press, 1965), p. 202. Although Schmidt's *Ursprung* is quoted in the bibliography, the authors do not discuss his ideas on Australian religion.

[42] From an old man, now dead—the last of his people to be

We must add that what, in the first quarter of the century, was called "All-Father," "High God," or "Supreme Being" is now being called, by some Australian ethnologists, "ancestral hero," "culture hero,"[43] or "sky hero," and "sky culture hero" (Elkin). A. P. Elkin does not seem to be as skeptical as the Berndts in regard to the earlier information about the Supreme Beings of southeast Australia. In speaking of Baiame, Daramulun, Nurunderi, Bunjil, and others, he asserts that they "bestowed on men their various items of material culture, gave them social laws, and above all, instituted the initiating rites. It is in the latter that the initiates first gain any real knowledge of him, and learn his secret name; even today civilized Aborigines will not breathe that name to the outsider."[44] But Elkin calls Baiame, Daramulun, and the others "sky heroes." They see and know everything and live in the sky, "a place often pictured as possessing much quartz crystal and fresh water." During his initiation the medicine man "can visit this sky land and see something

initiated—the Berndts collected a rather complete myth of Ngurunderi (of the lower Murray River in South Australia). The authors call Ngurunderi an "ancestral hero." He behaves like one; his myths consist of a series of travels and adventures, during which he shaped the land and performed some metamorphoses. "Finally he dived into the sea to cleanse himself of his old life and went up into the sky: Waieruwar, the spirit world. But before disappearing, he told the Jaraldi people that the spirits of their dead would always follow the tracks he had made, and eventually join him in the sky-world" (*ibid.*, p. 204). This last detail is important. Ngurunderi seems to represent a sky hero who preserved some traits of a celestial High Being.

[43] See R. M. and C. H. Berndt, *ibid.*, p. 141, with reference to Baiame and Daramulun.

[44] A. P. Elkin, *The Australian Aborigines* (1938; 3d ed., Sydney: Angus and Robertson, 1954; reprint, New York: Doubleday, 1964), p. 224.

of Baiame; and finally, the departed go there as they are
entitled to do by reason of their initiation" (*The Australian
Aborigines*, p. 224). The sky hero, Elkin continues, usually
was referred to by the aborigines as "father" or "all-
father," the bull-roarer was his symbol, and "he was and
is the sanction for essential laws, customs and rites" (p.
225).

One can readily see that Elkin's presentation of the south
Australian sky hero corresponds almost exactly to Howitt's
and Lang's description of the "All-Father" and to Graebner's "great god." Most probably the eminent ethnologist
hesitated to use these terms because of their ideological
and even theological connotations. As a matter of fact,
Elkin's "sky hero" is a real god—in his opinion, a mystery-
religion type of god: "As far as I can see the matter, and
I have discussed it with initiates, this sky-hero corresponds
to the hero of religious secret societies, the mysteries of
which go back to the old mystery cults of a few thousand
years ago, and with which I am prepared to believe that
this cult is historically connected, by whatever incidents it
was brought to the Australians" (p. 244).

We shall not discuss here Elkin's hypothesis of the historical connection between the mystery cults and the Australian initiation.[45] What is important for our endeavor is

[45] So far as I know, Elkin has never made explicit what he meant
by "the old mystery cults of a few thousand years ago." Eleusis?
Hellenistic mystery religions? But at the center of such mystery
cults were "dying and rising gods," not "sky heroes." Perhaps he
was thinking of Mithra, the only mystery god who does not know
death; but Mithra cannot be classified among the "sky heroes"
either. In his book *Aboriginal Men of High Degree* (Sydney:
Australasian Publishing Co., 1945), pp. 76–77, Elkin points out the
similarities between the parapsychological powers of the Australian

(1) that Elkin does not doubt the authenticity of the south-east Australian Sky Beings and (2) that he considers them to precede the totemic Heroes chronologically. Indeed, he writes:

Initiation and the secret life spread all over Australia and though now in central and northern parts of Australia, the belief in the sky-hero of initiation has either ceased to exist or else has been pushed into the background by the totemic heroes whose spirits are tied to the earth, yet a careful survey of the evidence suggests that initiation there, too, was possibly, in former days, a means of gaining knowledge of the sky-hero and access to his world. In the north-west, the heroes who taught the natives how to make the bull-roarer, and who introduced initiation ceremonies, belong to the sky. In an important

---

medicine man and the feats of the Indian and Tibetan yogis. He is inclined to accept a historical connection between them (see Eliade, *Birth and Rebirth*, pp. 99 ff.). We shall return to this problem later (see below, pp. 150 ff.). For the moment, let us add that there are also similarities between the medical ideas and practices of the Australian medicine men and those of the aboriginal tribes of India; see E. Drobec, "Heilkunde bei den Eingeborenen Australien," *Wiener Beiträge zur Kulturgeschichte und Linguistik*, IX (1952), 280–307; see p. 305. But such similarities do not imply an influence from the Indian or Tibetan yogis. Elkin also compares the initiatory pattern of the Australian medicine man to a mummification ritual attested in eastern Australia, which might represent a Melanesian influence (*Aboriginal Men of High Degree*, pp. 40–41). But Elkin is inclined to believe that Melanesian influences were bearers of ideas and techniques that had originated in higher cultures. Is Elkin connecting the initiation of the Australian medicine man with the Egyptian ritual of mummification? Such hypotheses would remind one of the "Egyptian diffusionism" of G. Elliot-Smith and W. J. Perry. In any case, it is an unwarranted hypothesis: the same pattern of initiation is to be found among the Siberians and North and South American shamans; see M. Eliade, *Shamanism: Archaic Techniques of Ecstasy* (New York: Pantheon, 1964).

and widespread Central Australian myth concerning incompletely formed beings, which I think refers to an initiation rite performed on candidates, the hero and operator came from the sky.[46]

Other central Australian myths seem to illustrate the same ontological and chronological sequence: Sky Beings—totemic Heroes. Already in 1904, Spencer and Gillen had described Atnatu, the Primordial Being of the Kaitish tribe (in central Australia, just north of the Aranda), as preceding the *alcheringa* times, that is, the epoch of the "creation." Atnatu "arose up in the sky in the very far back-past. . . . He made himself and gave himself a name." He has wives and sons, the sons also being named Atnatu. Because certain of his sons neglected his sacred services, he expelled them from the sky. These sons came down to earth and became the ancestors of men. Atnatu sent to men "everything which the black fellow has." He is described as "a very great man, black," conducts sacred services in which the bull-roarers swing, and punishes those mortals who do not sound the bull-roarers at the initiation ceremonies.[47]

"Amongst the western Aranda and Loritja," Elkin writes, "the dream-time heroes are said in some myths to have had formerly associations with the sky-world and access to it by way of a mountain. The sky-hero, however, caused this to sink and so the dream-time totemic heroes had to remain on earth."[48] This mythical tradition is important and de-

[46] Elkin, *The Australian Aborigines*, p. 224.

[47] B. Spencer and F. J. Gillen, *The Northern Tribes of Central Australia* (London: Macmillan, 1904), pp. 498 ff. Elkin, *The Australian Aborigines*, p. 225, rightly observes that these are the prototype of the rites performed on earth.

[48] Elkin, *The Australian Aborigines*, p. 225.

serves to be analyzed more closely. We shall utilize primarily the information published by T. G. H. Strehlow.[49] According to this author, it was believed in the Aranda-speaking areas that the earth and the sky had always existed and had always been the home of Supernatural Beings. The western Aranda believe that the sky is inhabited by an emu-footed Great Father (Knaritja), who is also the Eternal Youth (*altjira nditja*). He has dog-footed wives and many sons and daughters. "They lived on fruits and vegetable foods in an eternally green land, unaffected by droughts, through which the Milky Way flowed like a broad river; and the stars were their campfires. In this green land there were only trees, fruits, flowers, and birds; no game animal existed, and no meat was eaten. All of these sky dwellers were as ageless as the stars themselves, and death could not enter their home."[50] The "reddish-skinned" Great Father of the sky is in appearance as young as his children.[51] Strehlow then goes on: "Although I have not

---

[49] T. G. H. Strehlow, "Personal Monototemism in a Polytotemic Community" (hereinafter cited as "Personal Monototemism"), *Festschrift für Ad. E. Jensen*, II (Munich, 1964), 723–54; see also his *Aranda Traditions* (Melbourne: Melbourne University Press, 1947) and "La gémelité de l'âme humaine," *La Tour Saint-Jacques* (Paris, 1957), No. 11–12 (Numéro spécial sur la magie), pp. 14–23. Most of this information is already given, in a more condensed form, in C. Strehlow's works; see n. 51. But we prefer to follow T. G. H. Strehlow's presentation, if only for the fact that his first language was Aranda.

[50] T. G. H. Strehlow, "Personal Monototemism," p. 725.

[51] C. Strehlow found similar beliefs among the Kukatja (whom he calls "western Loritja") and Matuntara (whom he calls "southern Loritja"); they spoke of a Sky Being with a wife and a small child. Gillen, too, reported that among the eastern Aranda group of Alice Springs "the sky is said to be inhabited by three persons—a gigantic man with an immense foot shaped like that of the emu, a

recorded any traditions about emu-footed or dog-footed sky dwellers outside the Western Aranda territory, it is nevertheless true that everywhere in the Aranda-speaking area a firm belief was held that the power of death was limited to the earth, and that men had to die only because all connections had been severed between the sky and the earth." Strehlow reminds us that traditions about broken "ladders" have been found at many ceremonial sites. Among the lower southern Aranda there is a myth of a gigantic casuarina tree which, at the beginning of time, stood at a sacred site in the Simpson Desert and touched

woman, and a child who never develops beyond childhood" (quoted by T. G. H. Strehlow, "Personal Monototemism," p. 725). We do not have to take up the long discussion that followed C. Strehlow's discovery of the Sky Being Altjira among the Aranda and of Tukura among the Loritja; see C. Strehlow and M. von Leonhardi, *Mythen, Sagen und Märchen des Aranda-Stammes in Zentral-Australien,* Vols. I–IV (Frankfurt a.M.: Veröffentlichungen aus dem städtischen Völker-Museum, 1907–20). Spencer denied that there were such gods; he insisted that the Aranda spoke only of *Alcheringa,* i.e., of the mythical or Dream Time. But it was soon realized that both affirmations were fundamentally correct and did not contradict each other (in spite of Spencer's refusal to accept the existence of an Aranda Sky Being). As a matter of fact, C. Strehlow's Altjira is par excellence the being of the primordial, mythical Dream Time, *alcheringa.* One can only regret Spencer's malicious statement that C. Strehlow's material "had to be obtained orally from some of the old men who were Christianized members of the Mission" (*The Arunta: A Study of a Stone Age People,* Vol. I [London: Macmillan, 1927], Preface, p. ix). T. G. H. Strehlow rightly points out that his father's primary western Aranda informant was an exceptionally intelligent medicine man born about 1846, "whose prestige as an authority on the beliefs extended far beyond the Western Aranda area" and who "remained an inflexible champion of the old order throughout the years of C. Strehlow's stay at Hermannsburg" ("Personal Monototemism," pp. 723–24, n. 1; see *ibid.,* the biographies of the other informants).

the sky with its topmost branches. A few miles away there was another casuarina tree which was ready to provide a suitable ladder for men to climb to the sky. But the tree was cut down by certain mythical personages, and the bridge between earth and sky was destroyed forever. There is also the myth of the two Ntjikantja brothers, already related by Strehlow in his *Aranda Traditions:* after pulling up the spear on which they had climbed into the sky, the brothers uttered a death curse upon the earth dwellers.[52] The Ntjikantja brothers, like the sun, the moon, and the stars, emerged from the earth and wandered about on its surface doing the same sort of works as the other earth-born totemic ancestors. But while the majority of the totemic Ancestors finally returned into the ground, those who rose into the sky took on celestial bodies and knew neither decay nor death. The Ntjikantja brothers turned into the Magellanic Clouds.[53]

For Strehlow, "it is clear that it would be impossible to regard the emu-footed Great Father in the sky of Western Aranda mythology as a supreme Being in any sense of the word; for neither he nor his family ever exerted any influence beyond the sky" ("Personal Monototemism," p. 726). Indeed, these Sky Beings did not create or shape the sky; nor did they bring into existence either plants, animals, men, or the totemic Ancestors; nor did they inspire or control any of the Ancestors' activities. In sum, these Sky Be-

[52] T. G. H. Strehlow, *Aranda Traditions*, p. 78. He gives the curse of the brothers: "You miserable death-doomed wretches, all of you must die now! You may never return from the earth while you are living, and you may never return after you are dead" ("Personal Monototemism," p. 726).

[53] T. G. H. Strehlow, "Personal Monototemism," p. 726.

ings were not even interested in what happened on the earth. The evil-doers had to fear not the Great Father of the sky but the wrath of the totemic Ancestors and the punishment of the tribal authorities (*ibid.*). All of the creative and meaningful acts were effected by the earth-born totemic Ancestors. For this reason the myths and religious functions associated with these ancestors will detain us at length later on.

From the perspective of history of religions, the transformation of a Sky Being into a *deus otiosus* seems to have reached its farthest limits among the western Aranda. The next step could only be his falling into total and definitive oblivion. This probably did occur outside of the western Aranda territory, where Strehlow was not able to find any comparable beliefs in Sky Beings. But one can point out two characteristic traits even in this indifferent, otiose, and "transcendent" Great Father and Eternal Youth that range him among the Supreme Beings: (1) his immortality, his eternal youth, and his beatific existence; (2) his "ontological" and "chronological" precedence over the totemic heroes—he had been there in the sky for a long time before the emergence of the totemic Ancestors from under the earth. Moreover, the religious significance of the sky is repeatedly proclaimed in the myths of the celestial immortality of those heroes who were able to ascend into heaven, in the mythical traditions about "ladders" or trees connecting heaven and earth, and especially in the widespread Aranda belief that death came into being only because the communications between earth and heaven had been violently interrupted.

As is well known, similar beliefs are attested in many other archaic religions. The myth of a primordial communication with Heaven (through a mountain, tree, ladder, liana, etc.) and its subsequent interruption is related to the Ancestor's loss of immortality or of his original paradisal situation. A celestial Supreme Being is usually implicated in these fateful events. After the breaking of the communi-cations between Heaven and Earth the God retires, be-comes more or less a *deus otiosus*, and only a few privileged persons—shamans, medicine men, heroes—are able to ascend to heaven and meet him. Now, we do not know how much of this mythical theme was known to the Aranda. But the fact is that the religious prestige of heaven did continue to survive, particularly in the notion that immortality belongs to the celestial bodies and Sky Beings.

Noting that in Kaitish mythology "the sky-being existed before this dream-time," Elkin surmises: "This possibly represents the historical sequence in that area and indeed in all the central, northern and north-western regions. Initi-ation was at first admission to the beliefs and rites con-nected with the sky-hero, but later it included also admis-sion into cult-totemism with its myths of the dream-time heroes, which in many tribes, as far as our knowledge goes, ultimately overshadowed the former belief and associa-tions."[54] This would imply that at one time the Sky Being beliefs were more widely diffused in Australia. Their dis-appearance or transformation follows the general pattern of the withdrawal of a celestial *deus otiosus* and his eventual and final oblivion. But what is important here is that the religious function of the Dream Time heroes (or totemic Ancestors) becomes equivalent to that of the Sky Beings. As Elkin remarks: "Just as in central or north-western

[54] Elkin, *The Australian Aborigines*, p. 225.

Australia, to say a custom is *altjira, djugur, ungud,* etc., that is, dreaming, is to give it final and unimpeachable authority, so in eastern Australia, to say of a custom, 'Baiame say so' is to provide the same kind of sanction. Finally, the myths in which the sky-hero figures, perform the same aetiological, historical, and sociological function as do those of the dream-time heroes, and through their representation in symbol and rite, entry is gained to the sacred, life-giving world—but this time it is in the sky."[55]

Djamar, Nogämain

We shall return to this functional equivalence between the models revealed in the "dreaming period" and the injunction of the type "Baiame say so." For the moment, let us examine two other celestial Supreme Beings and their actual roles in the religious life of their respective tribes. The Bād, of the West Kimberley, revere a Supreme Being called Djamar. He has no father; but we do know the name of his mother. Djamar never married. It is said that he "walks with a dog."[56] One of Worms's informants told him: "Djamar made all things. . . . He is living in the saltwater under a rock. Where the sea is bubbling there Djamar lives."[57] But this means only that Djamar's first bull-roarer (called by the Bād *galaguru*) is still there, under the foam of the breakers. The young initiates are led to the stony bed of the creek and are shown the holes where Djamar had planted his bull-roarer. "Earnestly

[55] *Ibid.,* pp. 225–26. Elkin specifies that "the two sets of beliefs co-existed not only in Central Australia but also on the north coast of New South Wales" (p. 226, n. 4).

[56] E. A. Worms, "Djamar, the Creator," *Anthropos,* XLV (1950), 643–58; see p. 650.

[57] *Ibid.,* p. 655.

the old men impress on the youths the terrible force of the original *tjurunga*, by pointing out the baldness of the surrounding hills and the damaged bark of the trees struck by Djamar when he whirled the bull-roarer. It smashed the rocks of the foreshore" ("Djamar, the Creator," p. 643). After these events Djamar ascended to the sky, together with his *tjurunga*. From there "he watches the people and gives them the native law which we call *Djamara-mara*. He sees when a man kills another with a spear or boomerang" (p. 650). Nevertheless, despite his ascension, Djamar "remains in Ngamagun Creek, and in all places where his engraved *galaguru* are preserved. These are carefully hidden by the natives in hollow trees near the silent water pools by their tribal country" (p. 643). The myth of Djamar is revealed during the initiation ceremonies. On this occasion the old men go into the forest searching for the tree under which Djamar rested in the mythical times. (And once again we note how, through the ritual, the mythical time is reactualized and the original tree is made present.) From this tree the bull-roarers of the new initiates will be prepared.[58]

Djamar's nature as a High Being is also reflected in his relations to Culture Heroes. One of these Culture Heroes, Nalgabi, carried Djamar's *galaguru* to a neighboring tribe. Djamar walked with another Hero, Marel, to a certain place, where Marel remained and where he still lives. "Marel makes the secret songs, but for men only. He watches the young initiated men and teaches them the law

[58] *Ibid.*, pp. 650 ff. On the Bād initiation, see E. A. Worms, "Initiationsfeiern," *Annali Lateranensi*, II (1938), 179–80; *idem*, "Religiöse Vorstellungen und Kultur einiger nordwestaustralischer Stämme in fünfzig Legenden," *Annali Lateranensi*, Vol. IV (1940).

of Djamar" (p. 650). Another Culture Hero, Minan, made dances and the smooth black stone axes. He now lives at a certain place in Beagle Bay. "Djamar orders Marel and Minan. He is their boss" (p. 650). Finally, another Hero, Ninj, was told by Djamar to make fish traps out of sticks and stones. "He got his job from Djamar."[59]

Thus it would seem that Djamar can be compared to the southeastern Supreme Beings: he is creator, he revealed the moral laws, he charged a certain number of Culture Heroes with the task of civilizing the Bād and supervising their religious ceremonies; finally he ascended to the sky, and from there he still watches men's behavior. The only aspect of this complex that is not clearly attested among the southeastern High Gods is Djamar's relation to the *tjurunga*. Formally, this *tjurunga* is a "pictograph or metaphorical record on wood." Some of the incised marks represent Djamar himself, others figure objects used by him, or lesser Supernatural Beings. Only an initiate can "read" the drawings correctly. But the *galaguru* is not only a symbol of Djamar; it is also a replica of the original bull-roarer that Djamar deposited under the rock of Ngamagun. Now, that original bull-roarer also exists in the sky. This would seem to imply that Djamar *is* that original *galaguru* (see p. 650). The notion that a divine being is embodied in his *tjurunga* reminds us of the identification between the mythical Heroes (Ancestors) and specific *tjurunga* which is characteristic of the central Australian tribes—a conception we shall discuss later. For the moment it is important for us to emphasize the mystical plurality of Djamar's bodies. As

[59] Worms, "Djamar, the Creator," p. 650; see also E. A. Worms, "Djamar and His Relation to Other Culture Heroes," *Anthropos,* XLVII (1952), 539–60.

Worms points out, "wherever today an authorized replica of this *galaguru* is carved, carried or stored, there Djamar and his original location of Ngamagun is occasioned again. There his personal presence is obtained, repeated and multiplied. 'We cannot carry that rock to this place. Therefore we make this *djidi* (i.e. *tjurunga*)—and Djamar is here,'" said one of Worms's informants.[60]

We can surmise that Djamar was able to conserve his religious actuality particularly because of the ritual importance of the *galaguru,* which can be considered his "mystical body." The initiation consisted of the communication of Djamar's myths and the disclosure of his identity both with the celestial *galaguru* and with the primordial one buried under the rock at Ngamagun.

Our second example is taken from the Murinbata, a tribe of western Arnhem Land studied carefully and at great length by W. E. H. Stanner. The pattern of the Murinbata religious life is constituted by a series of events that took place in the "dreaming period." But there are also a number of "pure spirits" whose religious prestige is independent of that prodigious mythical period. The most eminent among them is Nogämain, "a sky-dweller, who lived (according to some) 'of his own will' or 'in his own fashion'— and alone, except for a dog, with 'no father, no mother, no brother, no child'; but (according to others) with a wife and son, the son being symbolized by a hunting spear. It was supposed to be Nogämain's influence at work, through his son, if a hunter killed a kangaroo or wallaby with one throw of a spear."[61] According to Stanner, some people

[60] Worms, "Djamar, the Creator," p. 657.
[61] W. E. H. Stanner, "On Aboriginal Religion, VI," *Oceania,* XXXIII (1963), 239–73; see p. 264 (also: Oceania Monograph No. 11, reprint, p. 162).

identified Nogämain with the man in the moon. Others were not so sure; when asked of his abode, they raised their arms toward the whole sky and said a single word: "on high." Thunder and lightning were attributed to "the people of Nogämain." He was also responsible for sending spirit children; Stanner heard many times: "Nogämain sends down good children." But he also received the same information about other "pure spirits." The most important cultic act was the prayer for food in case of distress; one of Stanner's oldest informants remembered that, as a child, he had heard the oldest men "calling out to Nogämain at night when they lay in camp short of food" ("On Aboriginal Religion," p. 264).

In Nogämain we have a clear example of a celestial god in the process of being supplemented by other Figures (Kunmanggur and Kukpi also send the spirit children) and on the point of losing his religious actuality (only one of the oldest informants remembered, from his childhood, the prayer of the oldest men). The discrepancies and contradictions among various descriptions of Nogämain, as remarked by Stanner, are an indication of his progressive religious irrelevance. In comparison with the Great Father of the western Aranda, Nogämain still preserves a certain religious actuality: for example, he cares for men. But unlike Djamar—or, we can surmise, Atnatu of the Kaitish—he does not play any important role in the initiation ceremonies.

Two Kinds of "Primordiality"

But apparently the irrelevance, the vagueness, or the absence of a celestial High Being does not modify the pan-Australian pattern of the religious life. As Elkin puts it: to say that a custom is *altjira,* "dreaming," is the same as to say of a custom: "Baiame say so." Elkin rightly insists on the chronological anteriority of the Sky Beings as compared with the Culture (or totemic) Heroes. As we know, the same opinion was held by Lang, Graebner, and Schmidt. But what is important in this process is that the religious function of the *primordial* and *primordiality* remains the same. Whatever the context may be—supernatural Sky Gods, Culture Heroes, Wondjina or Ungud (to be discussed in our next chapter)—the primordial mythical time has an overwhelming significance. Only that which was effected *in illo tempore* is real, meaningful, exemplary, and of inexhaustible creativity. Among the western Aranda we noted a passage from what might be called a "speculative" primordial time—the epoch of the celestial, eternal Great Father— to a primordial time rich in existential values, the fabulous epoch of the "dreaming" when the totemic Ancestors (or Culture Heroes) shaped the world, created the animals, and completed and civilized man. The "primordiality" of the Great Father was not of immediate relevance to the Aranda's existence; once the communication with heaven had been interrupted and death had come into the world, it was not very helpful to know about the immortality of Altjira's family or of those who had ascended to heaven. The only "immortality" accessible to the Aranda and to other Australian tribes was the reincarnation, the perennial return to life of the primordial Ancestors—conceptions we shall take up in a future chapter.

Thus it seems as if the pattern of Australian religions implies the substitution of a "primordial" directly related to the human condition for the "primordial" preceding this condition. Such a process is known in other religions too; we might refer, for example, to the "primordiality" of Tiamat and the passage to the creative primordial epoch represented by the victory of Marduk, the cosmogony, anthropogony, and the founding of a new divine hierarchy. Or we might compare the primordiality of Ouranos with the establishment of Zeus' supremacy—or point to the passage from the almost forgotten Dyaus to Varuna and later still to the consecutive supremacies of Indra, Shiva, and Vishnu.[62]

What is significant in this substitution of an "existential" primordiality for a "speculative" one is that this process represents a more radical incarnation of the *sacred* in *life* and *human existence*. We shall have an opportunity to illustrate this process when we examine the coming into being of the Aranda totemic Ancestors and the myths of the Australian Culture Heroes. The abundance of embryological imagery is not without a profound religious meaning. It is as if the entire grandiose cosmogonic drama were being interpreted in terms of procreation, pregnancy, embryonic existence, and obstetric operations. But none of these fabulous events is either "human" or "profane" in nature. They are primordial, creative, exemplary, and thus religious acts. Ultimately they represent mysteries which only the fully initiated men will be able to grasp.

[62] See also the discussion of a similar problem by Charles H. Long, "The West African High God: History and Religious Experience," *History of Religions*, III (Winter, 1964), 328–42.

CHAPTER 2

Culture Heroes and
Mythical Geography

For the Australians, as well as for other primitive societies, the world is always "their own world," that is to say, the world in which they live and whose mythical history they know. Outside this familiar cosmos lie amorphous, unknown, dangerous lands, peopled by mysterious and inimical ghosts and magicians. The aborigines dread an adventure, even in numbers, into unknown territories.[1] These strange lands do not belong to their "world" and consequently still partake of the uncreated mode of being.

Yet even the most arid and monotonous landscape can become a "home" for the tribe when it is believed to have been "created" or more exactly, transformed by Supernatural Beings. Giving shape to the land, the Supernatural Beings at the same time made it "sacred." The present countryside is the result of their work, and they themselves belong to a realm of being different from that of men. These Primordial Beings, moreover, not only molded the landscape; they also inserted in some places "spirit children" and "spirits" of various animals, brought forth from their own bodies.

The epoch when the Supernatural Beings appeared and began to transform the world, wandering across immense

[1] Elkin, *The Australian Aborigines,* pp. 38 ff., 49 ff.

42

territories, producing plants and animals, making man as he is today, giving him his present institutions and ceremonies —this epoch was the "Dream Time" or, as some authors call it, the "Eternal Dream Time" or just "Dreaming." This mythical time is "sacred" because it was sanctified by the real presence and the activity of the Supernatural Beings. But like all other species of "sacred time," although indefinitely remote, it is not inaccessible. It can be reactualized through ritual. Moreover, it constitutes "a kind of charter of things that still happen, and a kind of *logos* or principle of order transcending everything significant for aboriginal man."[2] Or, as Ronald and Catherine Berndt put it, "the mythological era . . . is regarded as setting a precedent for all human behavior from that time on. It was the period when patterns of living were established, and laws laid down for human beings to follow."[3]

Everything which fully *exists*—a mountain, a water place, an institution, a custom—is acknowledged as real, valid, and meaningful because it came into being *in the beginning*. In Chapter 1, we discussed the works of "creation" effected by the Sky Gods of the southeast Australian tribes; we also pointed out traces of a similar type of celestial divine Being

[2] W. E. H. Stanner, "The Dreaming," in T. A. G. Hungerford (ed.), *Australian Signposts* (Melbourne, 1956), pp. 51–65 (reprinted in William A. Lessa and Evon Z. Vogt, *Reader in Comparative Religion* [New York: Harper & Row, 1958], pp. 513–23; see p. 514). See also below, pp. 197 ff.

[3] R. M. and C. H. Berndt, *The World of the First Australians,* p. 188; see p. 187, for a list of Australian terms for "Dreaming." We have analyzed the structure and meaning of the necessity to relate all human behavior to paradigmatic precedents in our *Myth of the Eternal Return* (English trans., New York: Pantheon, 1954; reprinted as *Cosmos and History: The Myth of the Eternal Return* [New York: Harper & Row, 1959]).

in other parts of the continent. In southeast Australia, the *origins* are dominated by the creative activity of the Sky Gods ("All-Fathers"). We shall now examine at some length other Australian conceptions of the *beginnings*, in order to discover what type of Supernatural Beings dominated such fabulous, creative epochs.

The Aranda Myth of Origins

According to the Aranda, the earth in the beginning was like a desolate plain, without hills or rivers, lying in eternal darkness. The sun, the moon, and the stars were still slumbering under the earth. There existed no plants or animals, only semi-embryonic masses of half-developed infants, lying helplessly at places which were later to become salt lakes or water holes. These shapeless infants could not develop into individual men and women—but neither could they grow old or die. Indeed, neither life nor death was known on earth. "Only below the surface of the earth did life already exist in its fulness, in the form of thousands of uncreated supernatural beings that had always existed: but even these were still slumbering in eternal sleep."[4]

Finally these Supernatural Beings awakened from their sleep and broke through the surface of the earth. Their "birthplaces" were impregnated with their life and power. As the Sun too rose out of the ground, the earth was flooded with light. The Supernatural Beings that "had been born out of their own eternity" (*altjirana nambakala*) had various shapes and appearances. Some rose in animal

[4] T. G. H. Strehlow, "Personal Monototemism in a Polytotemic Community" (hereinafter cited as "Personal Monototemism), *Festschrift für Ad. E. Jensen*, II (Munich, 1964), pp. 723–54; see p. 727.

forms, like kangaroos or emus; others emerged as perfectly formed men and women. "In most of these supernatural beings there was an indivisible linking between elements found in animals (or plants) on the one hand and in humans on the other. Those beings that looked like animals, for instance, generally thought and acted like humans; conversely, those in human form could change at will into the particular animal with which they were indivisibly linked."[5]

These Supernatural Beings, commonly designated "totemic Ancestors," began to wander on the surface of the earth, giving the central Australian landscape its actual physical features. Some of them assumed the functions of "Culture Heroes." They "sliced massed humanity into individual infants, then slit the webs between their fingers and toes, and cut open their ears, eyes and mouths" (Strehlow, "Personal Monototemism," p. 728). Other Culture Heroes taught men how to make tools and fire and to cook food. When all these earthborn Supernatural Beings had accomplished their labors and completed their wanderings, "overpowering weariness fell upon them. The tasks that they had performed had taxed their strength to the utmost" (p. 728).

Thus they sunk back into their original slumbering state,[6] and "their bodies either vanished into the ground (often at the site where they had first emerged) or turned into rocks, trees, or tjurunga objects. The sites which marked their final resting places were, like their birthplaces, regarded as important sacred centres, and were called by the same name

[5] *Ibid.*, p. 727. This is, of course, a widely spread conception among the archaic hunters.

[6] But, although resting in perpetual slumber, they were aware of what went on on the earth (*ibid.*, p. 741).

—pmara kutata. Both kinds of *pmara kutata* could be approached only by initiated men, and only on special ceremonial occasions. At all other times they were places that had to be avoided on pain of death" (p. 729).

The disappearance of the Supernatural Beings put an end to the mythical age, which—at least in the case of the Aranda—had a somehow paradisal character. Indeed, the Ancestors "were free from the multitude of inhibitions and frustrations that inevitably obstruct all human beings who are living together in organized communities. Nor were they accountable for their actions to any superior Power. For they were personages living in a world where the human notions of good and evil had but a shadowy meaning: they wandered around 'beyond the borders of good and evil,' as it were."[7] This does not mean, however, that they were completely beyond all moral laws. T. G. H. Strehlow recalls certain myths showing that criminal acts did not remain unpunished.[8]

These primordial personages had a specific mode of being which, though different from that of men as they now exist, nonetheless constitutes its source and model. This is the reason for the immediate, "existential" interest of the Ancestors' myths for the Aranda—and also for their indifference to the Sky Beings. Indeed, unlike the Sky Beings, the Primordial Ancestors were subject to aging and decay. But, unlike present-day men, they were immortal; even

[7] *Ibid.*, p. 729. Cf. also Strehlow, *Aranda Traditions*, pp. 36 ff., on "the Golden Age" of the totemic Ancestors.

[8] Indeed, "there existed some indefinably nameless Force which was capable of bringing about the final downfall of even the most powerful supernatural beings that had believed themselves superior in strength to all possible opponents" (Strehlow, "Personal Monototemism," p. 729).

those who were "killed" by other totemic Ancestors have continued to live in the form of *tjurungas*. Nonetheless, before they finally sink into the earth, death has been brought into the world through some of their acts. Thus the first men come into existence in a world of labor, pain, and death.[9] But the "life" that is left behind by the Ancestors throughout the land assures continuity with the fabulous past. And what we call "religion" and religious activity is just that corpus of traditional techniques and rituals by means of which the contemporary Aranda succeeds in keeping himself in communication with the mythological past of his tribe.

As a matter of fact, this "communication with the mythical past" begins with the *conception* of every present-day man, that is, when the fetus receives the minute part of his totemic Ancestor's "life" that constitutes his "immortal" soul. As Strehlow has recently pointed out, the Aranda believe that every human being possesses two souls: the first, the mortal soul, comes into being with the fetus, as a result of intercourse between the parents; the second soul, a particle of the Ancestor's "life," is received by the pregnant woman. It is this second, immortal, soul that gives his physical characteristics to the individual and also creates his entire personality (p. 730). Thus one can say that every new conception also reiterates the primordial activity of the Ancestors: in the beginning, they found an amorphous,

---

[9] *Ibid.*, p. 729. Cf. Strehlow, *Aranda Traditions*, pp. 42 ff., for the myth of the origin of death. The first dead had begun to emerge slowly from his grave when Urbura, the magpie, thrust a heavy spear into his neck and stamped him back into the ground with his heel, shouting: "remain rooted down firmly for all time; do not attempt to rise again; stay forever in the ground!"

prehuman mass which they transformed into real human beings; after the disappearance of the Ancestors, particles of their "life" (i.e., immortal souls) penetrate the fetus (which is animated by the mortal souls) and actually *create* the complete man.

What is striking in this description of Strehlow's is the singular, one might almost say extravagant, mode of being of the Aranda's mythological Ancestors. Their ontological structure gives them a special place among the many types of Supernatural Beings known to the historian of religions. They are different from the celestial gods, although like them they are uncreated and immortal. Moreover, some of the earthborn Supernatural Beings—the Sun, Moon, and others—are said to have ascended to heaven and become planets and stars. This means that the earthborn "immortals" were able to become celestial immortals; they had only to climb to heaven. In the first chapter, we recalled certain traditions about such "climbing to heaven": in the beginning, communication with heaven was possible and even easy (by climbing a tree, a liana, a ladder); another myth clearly connects the origin of death to an interruption of the traffic between earth and heaven: two mythical Ancestors who had climbed to heaven afterward pulled up the spear and pronounced a death curse upon men (pp. 725–26). Thus one can say of the Aranda reports that there were originally three classes of Beings, all of them uncreated and immortal: (1) the celestial gods in heaven; (2) the Primordial Beings under the earth; (3) the Primordial Proto-Men on the earth. They are different in that the last two classes of Beings have passed through an indefinite period of slumbering; moreover the last, the Primordial Proto-Men, although uncreated, knew only an "embryonic" im-

mortality: when they truly became men through the ana-
tomical operations performed by certain Culture Heroes,
they lost their original condition of indefinite virtuality.

The ontological originality of the totemic Ancestors is
further emphasized by the fact that, though immortal, they
were exhausted by their creative works and sank again
under the earth—from where, strangely enough, they nevertheless can see and judge man's deeds. Moreover, as we
shall see, they could be "killed" by men (of course, mythological, primordial men) and, as a result of this murder, at
least a part of them (their "spirits") ascended to heaven and
became celestial bodies and phenomena.[10] Another characteristic of their mode of existence is their multiplicity and
their simultaneous presence on the earth.[11] An Ancestor
exists simultaneously: (*a*) under the earth, (*b*) in various
cosmic and ritual objects (rocks, waterfalls, *tjurungas*,
etc.), (*c*) as "spirit children," and finally as (*d*) the man

[10] Other myths tell how Primordial Beings climbed to Heaven
by means of a lance and ultimately became celestial bodies. Cf. M.
Eliade, "Notes on the Symbolism of the Arrow," in *Religions in
Antiquity. Essays in Memory of E. R. Goodenough* (Leiden,
1968), pp. 463–75.

[11] "The body of the Ulamba ancestor is shown at many points of
the route he once travelled: the main peak of Ulamba, the rock
from which he sprang into life, the sharp hill near the mountain
pass south of Ulamba, the great boulder which forms the lower
portion of the Ulamba sacred cave, and many other rocks elsewhere, are, each one individually, stated to be 'the body of the
Ulamba ancestor.' In addition, there is a *tjuringa* of him at Ulamba,
and others in different storehouses, and the natives still would not
have been troubled even for a moment by their number. The body
of the *tjilpa* chief Malbanka is (or was) to be found, as far as I
know, in form of a *tjuringa* in each one of the main caves which
are to be found along the far-flung trail which he and his sons
once travelled" (Strehlow, *Aranda Traditions*, pp. 28–29).

(or men) in which he is presently reincarnated. Now, it is a characteristic of religious thought in general, and of archaic thinking in particular, that Supernatural Beings are conceived as singular and unparalleled solutions of the unity-multiplicity problem. But what seems to be peculiar to the Australians is the mysterious connection between *their* land (i.e., mystical geography), the mythical history of that land (i.e., the deeds of the Ancestors), and man's responsibility for keeping the land "living" and fertile. All of this will become clearer as we proceed in our investigation. But we can already perceive that the ontological structure of the Primordial Beings (the mythical Ancestors) is so complex—more complex, for example, than that of the Sky Being (who is, in fact, a Supreme Being becoming a *deus otiosus*)—because they are involved in or incarnate the mysteries of life and fertility, of death and rebirth.

Numbakulla and the Sacred Pole

To understand better the paradigmatic creativity of these Primordial Beings, we shall discuss a few examples. In general the myths represent the Ancestors as powerful and creative. They can fly above and walk beneath the earth. They travel everywhere, performing sacred ceremonies and depositing "spirit children" in the ground or in various natural features. But their myths are seldom exuberant or dramatic. For example, Spencer and Gillen tell the following story of Numbakulla, whose name means "always existing" or "out of nothing." (This is one of the Supernatural Beings discussed by Strehlow [see p. 49 above], called *altjirana nambakala*, "born out of their own eternity"). According to the traditions of the Achilpa, one of the Aranda groups, Numbakulla arose "out of nothing" and traveled to the north, making mountains, rivers, and all sorts of animals and plants. He also created the "spirit children" (*kuruna*), a very large number of whom were concealed inside his body. Eventually he made a cave or storehouse, to hide the *tjurungas* that he was producing. At that time men did not yet exist. He inserted a *kuruna* into a *tjurunga*, and thus there arose the first Achilpa (mythical) Ancestor. Numbakulla then implanted a large number of *kuruna* in different *tjurunga*, producing other mythical Ancestors. He taught the first Achilpa how to perform the many ceremonies connected with the various totems.

Now, Numbakulla had planted a pole called *kauwa-auwa* in the middle of a sacred ground. (A representation of this pole, made from the trunk of a young gum tree, is erected on the ceremonial ground during the long series of initiation rites known as the Engwura). After anointing it with blood, he began to climb it. He told the first Achilpa Ancestor to follow him; but the blood made the pole too slippery, and the man slid down. "Numbakulla went on alone, drew up the pole after him and was never seen again."[12]

This pole is charged with important symbolism and plays

---

[12] Spencer and Gillen, *The Arunta*, I, 355 ff., esp. p. 360. Strehlow, *Aranda Traditions*, p. 78, quotes the west and south Aranda myth of the Ntjikantja Ancestors: the two brothers ascended into the sky by climbing up a tall spear (cf. above, p. 48). Spencer and Gillen, *op. cit.*, pp. 307 ff., relate another myth: the two Numbakulla made men from a living, embryonic substance (*inapatna*). Such a "Creation" of man by the metamorphosis of a prehuman element is indicated in the symbolic designs of the *tjurungas;* cf. L. Adam, "Anthromorphe Darstellungen auf australischen Ritualgeräten," *Anthropos,* LIII (1958), 1–50; see pp. 36 ff.

a central role in ritual. The fact that Numbakulla disappeared into the sky after climbing it suggests that the *kauwa-auwa* is somehow an *axis mundi* which unites heaven and earth. Elsewhere, and particularly in the Oriental cultures and the areas under their influence, the *axis mundi* (conceived as a pillar, a tree, a mountain, etc.) actually constitutes a "center of the world." This implies, among other things, that it is a consecrated place from which all orientation takes place. In other words, the "center" imparts structure to the surrounding amorphous space. Both the Achilpa myth and the actual ceremonial use of the pole illustrate very well this double function of communication with heaven and means of orientation. The myth relates in seemingly endless detail the wanderings of the first Achilpa Ancestors after the disappearance of Numbakulla. They traveled continuously, in small groups, carrying out ceremonies, circumcising the young men, occasionally leaving one of them behind. When these mythical groups performed the Engwura rituals, the *kauwa-auwa* "was always erected and made to lean in the direction in which they intended to travel."[13] In other words, the sacred pole helped them to chart the unknown space into which they were preparing to adventure.

One day an accident befell one of these mythical groups: while pulling up the *kauwa-auwa*, which was very deeply implanted, the old chief broke it just above the ground. They carried the broken pole until they met another group. They were so tired and sad that they did not even try to erect their own *kauwa-auwa* "but, lying down together, died where they lay. A large hill, covered with big stones,

[13] Spencer and Gillen, *The Arunta*, p. 382. On the ceremonial pole, cf. Strehlow, *Aranda Traditions*, pp. 77 ff.

arose to mark the spot."[14] Seldom do we find a more pathetic avowal that man cannot live without a "sacred center" which permits him both to "cosmicize" space and to communicate with the transhuman world of heaven. So long as they had their *kauwa-auwa*, the Achilpa Ancestors were never lost in the surrounding "chaos." Moreover, the sacred pole was for them the proof par excellence of Numbakulla's existence and activity.

The Myth of Bagadjimbiri

The creative deeds of such mythological heroes are equivalent to a cosmogony. The world came into being as a result of their work. In some cases, the cosmogonic character of the Dream Time activity is quite evident. This is true, for example, of the mythology of the Karadjeri tribe, which centers around the two brothers Bagadjimbiri. Before their appearance there was nothing at all—neither trees, nor animals, nor human beings. The brothers arose from the ground in the form of dingos, but they later became two "human" giants, their heads touching the sky. They emerged from the earth just before twilight on the first day. When they heard the cry of a little bird (*duru*) that always sang at that time, they knew it was twilight. Previously they had known nothing at all. The two brothers subsequently saw all kinds of animals and plants and gave them names. That is to say, from that moment, because they had names, the animals and plants began to *really* exist. Next the brothers saw a star and the moon and named them also.

[14] Spencer and Gillen, *The Arunta*, p. 388. For the meaning of this myth and its related ritual, cf. Ernesto de Martino, "Angoscia territoriale e riscatto culturale nel mito Achilpa delle origini," *Studi e Materiali di Storia delle Religioni*, XXIII (1952), 52–66.

Then the Bagadjimbiri went toward the north. On their journey they encountered men and women without genital organs, and the brothers provided them with organs made from a species of mushroom. They threw a *pirmal* (a long stick) at an animal and killed it; the Karadjeri found the stick and have performed the same act ever since. The two brothers founded the initiation ceremonies and utilized for the first time the ritual instruments: a stone circumcision knife, the bull-roarer, and the long *pirmal*. They saw a snake and sang the song for the production of snakes. Then they differentiated the dialects.

The two Bagadjimbiri had a great deal of hair, some of which they pulled out and gave to every tribe. (Thus every tribe now possesses a corporeal particle of the Heroes.) But a certain man killed the brothers with a spear. Their mother, Dilga, who was far away, detected the odor of corpses upon the wind. Milk streamed forth from her breasts and flowed underground to the place where the brothers lay dead. There it gushed like a torrent, drowning the murderer and reviving the two brothers. The two Bagadjimbiri later transformed themselves into water snakes, while their spirits became the Magellanic Clouds.[15]

This myth constitutes the foundation of all Karadjeri life. During initiation the ceremonies instituted by the two Bagadjimbiri are re-enacted, although the meaning of some

[15] Ralph Piddington, "Karadjeri Initiation," *Oceania*, III (1932–33), 46–87; *idem, An Introduction to Social Anthropology* (Edinburgh: Oliver & Boyd, 1950), pp. 91–105. The murder of Bagadjimbiri may be connected with another Australian mythical theme: a Culture Hero "kills" the young man during the initiation and is finally himself slain by the surviving members of the tribe; cf. B. Spencer, *Native Tribes of the Northern Territory of Australia* (London: Macmillan, 1914), pp. 214 ff., 270 ff., 295–305.

of the rituals is no longer clear to the aborigines. This mythical pattern is well known in different parts of Australia: the epiphany of the Culture Heroes, their wanderings and their civilizing activities, their final disappearance. As we shall see, every act of the Heroes (Ancestors) is duly repeated by the members of the tribe. As Strehlow put it: "All occupations originated with the totemic ancestors; and here, too, the native follows tradition blindly: he clings to the primitive weapons used by his forefathers, and no thought of improving them ever enters his mind."[16] But of course this is true only up to a certain point: the Australians, like other primitives, have changed their lives in the course of history; but all such changes are considered to be new "revelations" of Supernatural Beings.

A Mythical Geography

Through the initiation rites the neophyte is gradually introduced to the tribal traditions; he discovers all that happened *ab origine*. This "knowledge" is total—that is to say, mythical, ritual, and geographic. In learning what took place in the Dream Time, the initiate also learns what must be done in order to maintain the living and productive world. Moreover, a mythical—or mystical—geography is revealed to him: he is introduced to the innumerable sites where the Supernatural Beings performed rituals or did significant things. The world in which the initiate henceforth moves is a meaningful and "sacred" world, because Supernatural Beings have inhabited and transformed it. Thus it is always possible to be "oriented" in a world that has a sacred history, a world in which every prominent

[16] Strehlow, *Aranda Traditions*, p. 35.

feature is associated with a mythical event. W. E. H. Stanner writes, with regard to the Murinbata mythical geography: "The Murinbata considered the countryside filled with plain evidence that the dramas had occurred. The places of climax were known and named, and each one contained proof—a shape, or form, or pattern of a great event."[17] Likewise Spencer and Gillen, relating their journey to an important totemic center in the company of a small group of natives, disclose for us the mythical geography of the Warramunga tribe. A range of hills marked the path traversed by the mythical Ancestor of the bat totem. A column of rock represented another Ancestor, the opossum man; a low range of white quartzite hills indicated the white ant eggs thrown there in the Dream Time by some mythical women. "All the time, as we travelled along, the old men were talking amongst themselves about the natural features associated in tradition with these and other totemic ancestors of the tribe, and pointing them out to us."[18] And thus, during the three days of the journey, they passed near innumerable tangible traces of the Primordial totemic (cultural) Heroes. Finally they approached the famous water hole where the mythical snake Wollunka lived. Near the sacred pool the natives "became very quiet and solemn," and "the chief men of the totemic group went down to the edge of the water and, with bowed heads, addressed the Wollunka in whispers, asking him to remain quiet and do them no harm, for they were mates of his. . . . We could plainly see that it was all very real to them,

[17] W. E. H. Stanner, *On Aboriginal Religion* ("Oceania Monographs," No. 11, [Sydney, 1963]), p. 254.

[18] Spencer and Gillen, *The Northern Tribes of Central Australia*, p. 249.

and that they implicitly believed that the Wollunka was indeed alive beneath the water, watching them, though they could not see him."[19]

One must read the descriptions of Spencer and Gillen *in extenso* to understand why even the most dreary landscape is, for the aborigines, charged with awe: every rock, spring, and water hole represents a concrete trace of a sacred drama carried out in the mythical times. For the Western reader, these endless wanderings[20] and fortuitous meetings of the Dream Time Heroes seem excessively monotonous. (But then the wanderings of Leopold Bloom in *Ulysses* also seem monotonous for the admirer of Balzac or Tolstoi.) For the aborigines, the vestiges of the mythical drama are more than a cipher or stencil enabling him to read the sacred stories imprinted in the landscape. They reveal to him a history in which he is existentially involved. Not only is he the result of those endless wanderings and performances of the mythical Ancestors; in many cases he is the reincarnation of one of those Ancestors. As T. G. H. Strehlow puts it: "The whole countryside is his living, age-old family tree. The story of his own totemic ancestor is to the native *the account of his own doings at the begin ning of time*, at the dim dawn of life, when the world as he knows it now was being shaped and moulded by all-powerful hands. *He himself has played a part in that first glorious*

[19] *Ibid.*, pp. 252–53.
[20] The theme of the wanderings of the Ancestors appears to be characteristic of Australian mythology, but it is not exclusively Australian. It is found, for example, among the Californian Mohave (Yuman tribe); cf. A. L. Kroeber, *Handbook of the Indians of California* (Bureau of American Ethnology, Bull. LXXVIII [Washington, D.C., 1925]), pp. 754–57; *idem*, "Seven Mohave Myths," *Anthropological Records*, XI, No. 1 (1948), 4–8.

adventure, a part smaller or greater according to the original rank of the ancestor of whom he is the present reincarnated form" [italics mine].[21]

Learning the mythical history of the familiar countryside, the initiate experiences a sort of *anamnesis:* he remembers his coming into being in the primordial time and his most remote deeds: "At the time of birth the totemic ancestor who has undergone reincarnation is totally unaware of his former glorious existence. For him the preceding months have been a 'sleep and a forgetting.' If he is born as a boy, the old men will later on initiate him and reintroduce him into the ancient ceremonies which he himself had instituted in his previous existence."[22] Through his initiation, the novice discovers that he *has already been here*, in the beginning; he was here under the appearance of the mythical Ancestor. In learning the deeds of his mythical Ancestor, he learns about his own glorious pre-existence. Ultimately, he is taught to repeat himself such as he was *ab origine;* that is to say, he is to imitate his own exemplary model.

We shall have an opportunity to take up this problem again in the course of our investigation. For the moment, it seems relevant for us to point out the Platonic structure of the Australian doctrine of *anamnesis*. As is well known, for Plato learning is recollecting; to *know* is to *remember* (cf. *Meno* 81). Between two existences on earth, the soul contemplates the Ideas: it shares in pure and perfect knowledge. But when the soul is reincarnated, it drinks of the spring of Lethe and forgets the knowledge it had obtained from its direct contemplation of the Ideas. Yet this knowl-

[21] Strehlow, *Aranda Traditions*, pp. 30–31.
[22] *Ibid.*, p. 93.

edge is latent in the man in whom the soul is reincarnated, and it can be made patent by philosophical effort. Physical objects help the soul to withdraw into itself and, through a sort of "going back," to rediscover and repossess the original knowledge that it had possessed in its extra-terrestrial condition. Hence death is the return to a primordial and perfect state, which is periodically lost through the soul's reincarnation.[23]

Of course, there can be no question of assimilating the Australian conception to Plato's doctrine of *anamnesis*. But it is significant that the belief in the perpetual reincarnation of the Ancestors has forced the Aranda to elaborate a theory of *anamnesis* fairly close to that of Plato. For Plato as well as for the Aranda, physical objects help the soul to *remember his real identity*. With this difference: for Plato, the soul through death is able to contemplate the Ideas, and thus to partake in Knowledge. For the Aranda, the knowledge in question is not philosophical but mythical and "historical": that which the novice discovers through initiation is what he did *in illo tempore;* he learns not ideas but his own primordial deeds and their meaning. He discovers in the mythology of a certain Hero his own fabulous biography. Certain physical objects (rocks, *tjurungas*, etc.) reveal themselves as proofs of his first and glorious existence on earth. For Plato, the physical objects help the soul to recover the knowledge of his extra-terrestrial condition. But for both Plato and the Aranda, the true *anamnesis* is the effect of a spiritual activity: philosophy for the Greek philosopher, initiation for the Australians.

[23] M. Eliade, *Myth and Reality* (New York: Harper & Row, 1963), p. 124.

The Rituals That "Re-create" the World

Thus the Aranda geography reveals a structure and a meaning because it is charged with mythical history. Even the geographical orientation is related to a mythical history. The aborigines follow the paths marked out by the Supernatural Beings and the mythical Ancestors. They seldom approach a sacred site by the shortest route; rather they deem it necessary to walk on the same path taken by the Supernatural Being connected with it.[24] The mythical history that transformed a "chaotic land" into a sacred and articulated world helps, moreover, to bind together groups and tribes. The paths pass through the "worlds" of different tribes, and between these tribes there is a "secret bond of friendship and a mutual claim to hospitality and protection."[25] The members of a cult group can travel safely along the path of the Hero even in other tribal territories. Each cult group is the custodian of a particular episode of the myth and of the particular rites associated with it. "But as continuity with the past, a full knowledge of social and ritual sanctions, and a complete assurance for the present and future can only be maintained and gained by a knowledge of the myth as a whole and the performance of all the rites, it is essential that each 'lodge' should do its part. Thus the groups and tribes are linked together by the cult-life."[26]

Though apparently confined to familiar territory, the "world" of a tribe is conceived as being all-embracing. Owing to the Australian kinship system, everybody is—or

[24] Elkin, *The Australian Aborigines*, p. 153.
[25] *Ibid.*
[26] *Ibid.*, p. 124.

can be—related to everybody else. If a friendly stranger approaches a camp, he is always finally recognized as being related to someone of the group. Consequently, for the Australians, only one "world" and only one "human society" exist. The unknown regions outside familiar lands do not belong to the "world"—just as unfriendly or mysterious foreigners do not belong to the community of men, for they may be ghosts, demonic beings, or monsters.

But the "world" must be kept alive and productive. By themselves, men have no power to "save" the world, to keep it indefinitely as it was "in the beginning," full of useful plants and animals, with creeks and rivers and with the rains coming at the right time. But men have been instructed to do what the Supernatural Beings and Heroes did during the Dream Time period. All of the ceremonies are only reiterations of these paradigmatic acts. The ritual reactualization of the mythical history reactivates communication with the Dream Time, regenerates life, and assures its continuation.

In short, the ritual "re-creates" the world. The wanderings and the actions of the Ancestral Heroes are re-enacted in long and tedious ceremonies. The so-called increase ceremonies (*intichiuma*), which center about the vegetable and animal foods—yams or lily roots, kangaroos, snakes, birds—assure the renewal of the species through a ritual repetition of their creation in the Dream Time. The renewal of the edible species, animal and vegetable, is tantamount to a "world renewal." This should not surprise us, for the "world" is first of all the land where the man *lives*, where he finds his food and shelter. As we shall later discover in a more detailed way, alimentation has a sacramental value.

In absorbing his food, the "primitive" partakes in the sacredness of the world. *Living as a human being* is in itself a *religious act*. For men assume the responsibility of preserving the world as it was made by the Supernatural Beings, periodically regenerating the world through rituals, and especially through the "increase ceremonies."

Some of these increase ceremonies are slight and mechanical, others, on the contrary, are quite dramatic.[27] For example, it has happened that a particular mythical Being performed increase ceremonies at a certain site, leaving a stone as storehouse for a specific animal life or spirit. "Another place on his journey might have been sanctified and made efficacious by the loss of some of his blood or part of his body, or by his body being transformed into stone. Such a site is henceforth sacred. It is a channel from the creative and eternal dream-time. The creative power is brought into operation and causes the increase, for example, of kangaroos, by the care bestowed on, and the rituals performed at, the site."[28] The performers say: "Let there be plenty of kangaroos here and there." But they also "blow powder from the stone, throw stones from the sacred heap, or take a mixture of powdered stone or earth and blood from the sacred place and deposit it in the countries where an increase of the species is desired and should normally occur. . . . The sacred stone or heap is not, for them, just stone or earth. It is in a sense animated; life can go forth from it."[29] As we shall later see (p. 82), the various acts of

[27] R. M. and C. H. Berndt, *The World of the First Australians*, pp. 227–31. See the elaborate description of the *intichiuma* ceremonies in Spencer and Gillen, *The Northern Tribes of Central Australia*, pp. 167 ff., 283 ff. See also below, p. 82.

[28] Elkin, *The Australian Aborigines*, p. 199.

[29] *Ibid.*, p. 200.

the "increase" ritual reiterate exactly the gestures of the Ancestors.

Redeeming Symbols

The increase ceremonies are apparently simple and monotonous. But for the initiates a seeming simplicity sometimes hides a very complex symbolism. And this is true of all Australian rituals. To give a single example: in northeastern Arnhem Land an emblem signifying a goanna's tail and vertebrae is ritually exhibited during a certain ceremony.

Totemic designs are painted down its trunk, and feathered pendants attached. Slowly the actor removes it from its shade, posturing as he does so; he writhes along the ground, holding the sacred stick close to his breast. Singing continues; he is revealing one of the mysteries to participant-onlookers, all highly-initiated men.

What does this mean? Here is an emblem which is a symbol of a goanna's tail and vertebrae, withdrawn from its shade. But to the neophyte it is much more than this. The shade or hut symbolizes a special conically-shaped mat, brought by the Djanggawul Fertility Mothers from a spirit land away in the sunrise, beyond the Morning Star. This mat is really a womb. When the goanna tail emblem is removed from it on the sacred ground, this signifies that the first people, ancestors of the present-day eastern Arnhem Landers, are being born from their Mother; and they, in turn, are associated with a combination of fertility symbols. Actually, there is symbol within symbol, meaning within meaning, much of it connected with fundamental drives.[30]

[30] R. M. and C. H. Berndt, *The First Australians* (Sydney: Ure Smith, 1952), pp. 78–79.

We meet here some new religious ideas (the Mother, the womb), about which we shall have more to say. But this example shows us how, in the guise of a very simple ritual, a rich mythology can be disclosed to the initiates and, consequently, how the connection with a spiritual world is maintained and reinforced. The disclosure of the sacred history of the tribe sometimes takes many years. Step by step, the individual becomes aware of the greatness of the mythical past. He learns how to relive the Dream Time through the ceremonies. Eventually he shall be completely immersed in the sacred history of his tribe; that is to say, he shall know the origin and understand the meaning of everything from rocks, plants, and animals to customs, symbols, and rules. As he assimilates the revelation conserved in the myths and rituals, the world, life, and human existence become meaningful and sacred—for they have been created or perfected by Supernatural Beings. At a certain moment in his life, a man discovers that before his birth he was a spirit and that after his death he is to be reintegrated into that prenatal, spiritual condition. He learns that the human cycle is part of a larger, cosmic cycle; the Creation was a "spiritual" act which took place in the Dream Time, and, although the cosmos is now "real" or "material," it nonetheless must be periodically renewed by the reiteration of the creative acts that occurred in the beginning. This renovation of the world is a spiritual deed, the result of a reinforcing communication with the "Eternal Ones" of the Dream Time.

In a similar fashion, human existence begins and ends—provisorily—in a spiritual world. As the Berndts put it: "To begin with, the essence of man or woman is purely spiritual. After birth . . . it takes on a materialistic form: but it never loses its sacred quality. Woman possesses this sacredness almost without any effort—especially in such places as northeastern Arnhem Land: but for man the accent is on ritual, and organized ceremony. For both, sacredness increases with advancing age; and at death they become, again, completely spiritual."[31]

Should the sacred ceremonies be neglected and the social customs despised, the world will regress to the darkness and chaos that existed before the Dream Time and the coming of the Supernatural Beings.[32] As a matter of fact, the "world" of the aborigines has already been almost destroyed by acculturation, and the survivors linger on in a life of frustration and sterility. "A camp without ceremonies, where moonlit evenings are silent, or broken only by the muttering of the card-players or a sudden burst of quarreling, is a camp where the people's zest for living has been lost or diverted into other or less satisfying channels. Where sacred ritual has been allowed to lapse, people no longer maintain conscious contact with their own traditions and background: and once this vital link has been broken, the whole course of their lives must reflect the change."[33]

Of course this is not yet the physical destruction of the cosmos presaged by the myths. But the result is almost the same: as the old "world" created or perfected by the Supernatural Beings becomes meaningless through acculturation, it is progressively obliterated. The survivors of this spiritual cataclysm will have to rebuild their culture with other means and new materials. The crystallization of a new Aus-

---

[31] *Ibid.*, p. 59.

[32] Cf. Helmut Petri, "Das Weltende im Glauben australischer Eingeborenen," *Paideuma*, IV (1950), 349–62.

[33] R. M. and C. H. Berndt, *The First Australians*, pp. 98–99.

tralian culture is still a thing of the future. But the degeneration and ruin of traditional values as a result of encounters with Western culture is a general phenomenon among "primitives." We shall have many occasions to point out the distortion, the hybridization, and the oblivion undergone by the most archaic religious ideas and beliefs. We shall also have an opportunity to analyze some new religious and cultural creations, born from the tragic encounter with Western values.

For the moment it suffices for us to emphasize the Australian's need to live in a *real* "world." This means an articulated, significant, resourceful land, formed, enriched, and consecrated by Supernatural Beings. Such a "world" has a "center" or a structure—and for this reason it is "oriented," it is not a chaos, an amorphous, bewildering vacuity. The coming into being of the world, of plants and animals and men, is the result of a sacred history scrupulously preserved in the myths and periodically reiterated in the secret ceremonies. This implies not only that the world has a "history"—a sacred history unfolded during the Dream Time—but also that man has assumed the responsibility for maintaining the world, by continuously re-enacting the stupendous events of the beginning and by endlessly infusing the land with the powers of "Dreaming." When man ceases to communicate with the Dream Time and to re-enact his mythical history, the world will disintegrate and life will wither, to disappear eventually from the surface of the earth.

Again and again we shall encounter Australian religious creations which have sprung forth from such fundamental conceptions. But they are never exactly the same. From tribe to tribe, from culture to culture, there are significant variants, shifts of perspective, brilliant innovations. No living culture is able to repeat itself indefinitely, for the simple reason that no culture endures in absolute isolation. The meeting of cultures, even of kindred forms which have issued from the same matrix, always provokes creative, if sometimes minute, innovations.

Thus there exists no culture without history, without changes and transformations brought on by external influences. But this "history" is not acknowledged as such by the primitives; although they are aware of the modifications that have taken place in a more or less remote past, they telescope these modifications into a primordial and ahistorical time and interpret them as the acts of mythical Beings. In sum, by the simple fact that the innovation has been accepted and absorbed into the traditional pattern, it is considered to have taken place in the Dream Time period.

Theogony and Mythology of the Unambal

We shall now present, in some detail, the religious traditions of the Unambal, a tribe of northwest Australia. The German ethnologist Andreas Lommel has published a clear and well-articulated monograph on these people,[34] whose mythology and religious customs differ in several respects from the patterns found in southeast and central Australia. These differences illustrate the complexity and richness of the Australian religious experience. But they are also important for another reason: they reflect certain historical changes, which we shall consider at the end of our investigation.

The Unambal begin any narrative related to their life,

[34] Andreas Lommel, *Die Unambal: Ein Stamm in Nordwest-Australien* (Hamburg, 1952).

their customs, or their myths by recounting the beginnings
of the world. This is a practice found among many other
primitive peoples and shows the importance of the creative
happenings of the primordial time. Thus, in the beginning,
say the Unambal, only earth and heaven existed. Deep in
the earth lived—and even now lives—Ungud, in the form of
a great snake. Ungud is often identified with the earth, but
also with the waters. In the sky lives Wallanganda, who is
lord of heaven and at the same time personifies the Milky
Way. Wallanganda is supposed "to have made everything."
He threw water on the earth, but Ungud "made the water
deep," and so it started to rain. Thus began life on earth.[35]

Together, Wallanganda and Ungud created everything,
but only during the night, as the outcome of a creative
dream. Ungud transformed himself—or herself, for Ungud
can be of either sex or even bisexual—into the Beings which
he dreamed. Similarly, Wallanganda "dreamed" the Beings
which he begot. He threw out from heaven a "spiritual
force" and shaped it into images. Afterward, he projected
these images, painted red, white, and black, onto the rocks
and caves, where they can still be seen. This, according to
the Unambal, was the origin of the painted images of
plants and animals. These pictures also constitute the "spiritual centers" of the Beings which they represent. The relation between the images and the beings depicted is said to be
that of "father and brothers." Only after molding the "spiritual force" of the Beings into their respective images did
Wallanganda make them *in concreto* and send them all
over the land. Wallanganda painted the beings without
mouth or eyes (these organs were later given by Ungud).
Wallanganda continues to beget, incessantly, sending "spir-

[35] *Ibid.*, p. 10.

itual germs" on the earth. He does not let his creatures die.[36]

On the rocks and cave walls, by the side of the reproductions of plants and animals, there are also anthropomorphic images, without mouths, which are called Wondjina. They personify the rain. According to the Unambal, the Wondjina were first found by Ungud, in a "creative dream," at the bottom of the waters. For this reason, every river, lake, or well belongs to a specific Wondjina image located in the neighborhood. Immediately after coming into being the Wondjina went forth upon the earth, bringing the rains and changing the landscape, making hills and plains.[37] While "the stones were still wet," the Wondjina built great "stone houses." (This, incidentally, indicates a megalithic tradition.) Then the Wondjina lay down on the "wet rocks," and their "impressions" produced the first rock paintings. The Wondjina entered the earth where their images are found today; they have subsequently lived under the earth, in the waters belonging to the rock paintings. There they incessantly create new "child germs."

According to the Unambal, every man begins as a "child germ," called *jallala*. His father finds him in a dream and in another dream projects him into his wife. This *jallala* is in fact a portion of a Wondjina living in a certain water place; but it is equally a fragment of Ungud. When a *jallala*

---

[36] *Ibid.*, pp. 11–12. According to other versions of the myth, it was not Wallanganda who made the rock paintings but the bird Kujon, at his order. Wallanganda projected from heaven the "spiritual force" of the Beings, and Kujon painted them gradually as he grasped these messages in his creative dream. Cf. *ibid.*, p. 12.

[37] See other myths about the Wondjina in *ibid.*, pp. 15 ff. Cf. also below, p. 76.

takes human form it is called *jajaru* and represents the "Ungud part" of the individual, or that portion of his soul which is descended from Ungud. Often the *jajaru* is said to be located in the kidneys; at death it goes back to the water hole and there awaits a new incarnation.[38]

There is a close relationship between a man and his place of "spiritual" origin. Generally speaking, one is always descended from the same Wondjina and the same water place as one's father. Thus there is always a certain number of individuals sharing the same spiritual origin. They are the rightful possessors of the region in which the water place and its respective Wondjina image are located. The oldest individual is considered to be the proper incarnation of the Wondjina. In speaking of his Wondjina this old man uses the first person: "As I came along in the Dream Time and I left my impression on the rock. . . ." He has the duty of repainting periodically, before the rainy season, the image of the Wondjina on the rock wall. He says: "I am going now to refresh and invigorate myself; I paint myself anew, so that the rain can come." He uses red ochre, white and yellow colors, and charcoal. After finishing his repainting he takes some water into his mouth and blows it on the rock image. In this manner, say the Unambal, the Wondjina brought rain in the Dream Time.

Near the anthropomorphic Wondjina are images representing plants and animals. As a matter of fact, the plant and animal totems are derived from the same "spiritual"

---

[38] Lommel, *Die Unambal,* p. 13. A man is supposed to have other souls, whose origin is unknown to the present-day Unambal. One of these souls is the "shadow" which, after death, goes to the land of the dead and preserves there a sort of postexistence. See also *ibid.,* p. 39 (the destiny of the souls after death).

source as man. Thus the aborigines live in an organic relationship with all nature. When mankind dies, the Wondjina
will also die, and therefore the animals will no longer increase, the rain will no longer fall, and the vegetation will
dry up. In short, the "world" will regress to the pre-crea-
tion "chaos."

Like many other Australian tribes the Unambal not only
are divided into two exogamous classes but also apply this
"dualistic" system to the entire world, spiritual as well as
natural. From primeval times, Ungud, Wondjinas, men,
animals, and plants have belonged to one of two classes.
The classes are named after the cranelike bird Kuranguli
and the wild turkey Banar. These mythical birds are two
Culture Heroes, who, after taking human form, founded
all the rules and institutions. Everything that they did in
the mythical time must be done again and again by the
Unambal. The myth of the Culture Heroes somewhat
parallels that of Wallanganda and Ungud. It is said that
they came from heaven, that they are self-created, that they
are the two Ungud snakes. Moreover, the first Wondjinas
were nothing other than forms of the Culture Heroes.
From them the first men descended; the first Ungud souls
were made by them. Kuranguli is more beautiful and more
intelligent than Banar, who is in fact rather stupid. For this
reason, they frequently enter into conflict[39]—a mythological
theme that is widely diffused.

Through the initiation rites, particularly the rites of circumcision and subincision, the adolescent is progressively
introduced into this mythical tradition. As everywhere else
in Australia, men immerse themselves more deeply in the

[39] *Ibid.*, p. 20.

world of myths as they grow older. The medicine man is the main factor in renewing communication with the primeval times. His role in the spiritual life of the tribe is considerable. In the medicine man the creativity of the Dream Time is kept alive. While in *extasis* he is able to send his soul to Ungud. We shall learn more of his powers when we discuss the problem of the Australian medicine man (Chapter 4).

Unambal and Ungarinyin

As is the case with every other Australian tribe, one can discern in the Unambal traditions some basic common elements, which can be considered pan-Australian, persisting side by side with more specific conceptions and beliefs. It suffices for us to examine the traditions of the neighboring Ungarinyin in order to see how the religious conceptions vary from one tribe to the next. Fundamentally, the Unambal and the Ungarinyin partake of the same religious pattern. But it appears that some beliefs have been either lost or radically modified by the Ungarinyin; or such variant beliefs can be interpreted as innovations introduced by the Unambal into an earlier pattern common to both tribes.

Like the Unambal and other Australian groups, the Ungarinyin believe in a mythical primordial time (*lálan*), when Creation took place.[40] The Ungarinyin also know Ungud (the Rainbow Serpent) and the anthropomorphic and celestial Wálangala; but the structures and functions of these figures are different. Wálangala is not a creator. The Ungarinyin believe that the Creation is the work of Ungud and the Wondjina. Ungud sent the sweet water from

[40] Helmut Petri, *Sterbende Welt in Nordwest-Australien* (Braunschweig, 1954), pp. 98 ff.

heaven and created the first ancestral couple in the waters. Wálangala can be considered as both a celestial god and a Culture Hero. He founded all the social and cultural institutions—and particularly the initiation rituals. The neophyte is taught the myths of Wálangala during the most secret phase of the ceremony. Wálangala is now in heaven; he sends the spirit children and watches to see whether the rules prescribed by him in the *lálan* time are being respected. If they are not, Wálangala will send a flood.

In short, Ungud is the creator of life in all of nature, and Wálangala is the author of the spiritual part of man. But one cannot say that Wálangala is an anthropomorphic Sky God and Ungud a theriomorphic primeval deity. Ungud, too, ascended to heaven at the end of the primordial time. And some myths assert that Wálangala was anthropomorphic while on earth but became a serpent in heaven. As Helmut Petri has noted,[41] this is not felt as a contradiction by the aborigines. Many Wondjina take on a serpentine aspect at the end of Creation, without losing their anthropomorphic qualities.[42]

Many things remain obscure about Wálangala. He can certainly be compared with the celestial Supreme Beings ("All Fathers") of the southeastern tribes; but no prayers are addressed to him (as is the case with Mungan-ngaua and Baiame), and nothing is said of his omniscience or his benevolence. It is possible, as Petri suggests,[43] that an original creative deity has split into two divine personages, but we do not have the necessary data to deal with this problem.

[41] *Ibid.*, p. 116.
[42] We have here one of the most archaic expressions of the snake as the symbol of virtuality.
[43] Petri, *Sterbende Welt*, p. 116.

Directly related to Wálangala is another Sky Hero, Ngúnyari, who plays an important role in the initiation ceremonies. Ngúnyari is supposed to have made the bull-roarers "with his blood and elbows" and to have put his voice in them. He also painted the bull-roarer with lightning motifs—which is another way of saying that the bull-roarer *is* the thunderbolt. Ngúnyari determined all the injunctions having to do with the bull-roarers (they must be hidden in caves, far from women and children, etc.).[44] After a series of wanderings, during which he revealed the mysteries of the bull-roarer to the aborigines, he ascended to the sky by means of a ladder. Now his shadow can be seen near Wálangala, on the Milky Way.[45]

Ngúnyari is still remembered by the old men of the tribe, but his bull-roarer and its cult already belong to the past. They were supplanted by another type of bull-roarer, similar in form to the central-Australian *tjurunga*. These bull-roarers "belong" to a new cult, Kurangara, about which more will be said later (pp. 172 ff.).[46]

There are also other Culture Heroes: Bánar and Kuránguli, known also by the Unambal; Wódoi and Djúngun, two small night birds who, after their work in the primeval

---

[44] *Ibid.*, pp. 119 ff.

[45] *Ibid.*, p. 118. A. Capell found the Ngúnyari myth also among the Unambal and the Gwiini, but without the story of his wanderings in the west; cf. "Mythology in Northern Kimberley, North-West Australia," *Oceania*, IX (1939), 382–402; see p. 396.

[46] Petri thinks that, among the Ungarinyin, Ngúnyari and the bull-roarers are of recent origin. They were introduced from the East. But it is impossible for us to know what type of cult objects were previously in use and supplanted by Ngúnyari and his bull-roarers. The aborigines, naturally, assert that Ngúnyari and the bull-roarers were with them "from the very beginnings" (Petri, *Sterbende Welt*, p. 128).

time, ascended to heaven and became the two stars Alpha and Beta Gemini;[47] many mythical Ancestors; and finally Kálura, who is associated with rain and with spirit children and can be considered the last important figure of the mythical lore of the tribe.[48]

We see, then, how the traditions of two neighboring tribes can vary. We also see how a cult can disappear almost under our eyes to be replaced by a more dramatic and aggressive one (Kurangara); this process must be kept in mind in analyzing the different layers of the Australian religions. But for the moment another feature commands our attention—a feature which, though characteristic of the Unambal and Ungarinyin, is not limited to them. We have noted that the structure and function of Wálangala is repeated in Ngúnyari and in other Culture Heroes. All of them are supposed to have founded the tribal culture and especially to have revealed the initiation rites. One has the impression that a *specific paradigmatic model is being repeated again and again, as if a certain type of mythological figure and a certain religious function must be continuously reactualized, made present, active, and efficient.* One encounters the same phenomenon in other primitive cultures.

Related to this process of reproducing the type and function of a Supernatural Being in a series of successive personages, one notes a contrary process of *reintegrating a multitude of mythical persons in a single divine figure.* The Ungarinyin believe that at the end of the Dream Time the

[47] Like Bánar and Kuránguli, these two Heroes are different and antagonistic: one does everything in the correct way, the other one is stupid and inefficient. They fought together and Wódoi killed Djúngun, from whose blood ochre originated.

[48] Petri, *Sterbende Welt*, pp. 132 ff., 139 ff.

Wondjina entered the earth and became Ungud. Thus Ungud, the serpent, is conceived both as a unity and as the totality of an indefinite number of Wondjina.[49] From a certain point of view one might speak of the procession or emanation of a divine principle, followed by the reintegration of these multiple hypostatizations. Even if this process were the result of the mingling of two or more cults, originally unrelated, the fact remains that the aborigines were able to deal successfully with such a paradoxical theory. The conception of Ungud as being simultaneously a unity and a totality of numberless separate individuals is not exceptional among the Australians. We have already noted that the Aranda point to the body of their mythical Ancestor in all of the places where he traveled. They believe "in the simultaneous presence of the ancestor at each of the many scenes which once witnessed the fulness of his supernatural powers."[50]

The Wondjina and the Rainbow Serpent

Most of the beliefs of the Unambal and the Ungarinyin are also to be found, with the inevitable variations, among the other tribes of northern Kimberley and Arnhem Land. The paintings of the caves and rock shelters of northern Kimberley[51] both depict the mythology of the tribe and at

[49] *Ibid.*, p. 147. Cf. also T. Hernández, "Myths and Symbols of the Drysdale River Aborigines," *Oceania*, XXXII (1961–62), 113–27, for similar conceptions of the Ungur and Wondjina (Galoru) among a population of northern Kimberley.

[50] Strehlow, *Aranda Traditions*, p. 29.

[51] On March 26 and 27, 1838, Lieutenant George Grey discovered two caves containing paintings (cf. the description and colored sketches in his *Journals of Two Expeditions of Discoveries* (London, 1841), I, 201–4, 213–15). Many other caves with similar

the same time serve as a means for reanimating the contact with the Dream Time. Each gallery includes representations of various species of animals and at least one anthropo-

---

rock paintings were explored, described, and photographed by F. S. Brockman (1901), H. Basedow (1916), and W. R. Easton (1921). In 1928, Elkin visited three sets of cave and rock-shelter paintings of the Ungarinyin and for the first time presented in a coherent way their relations to the religious, economic, and social life of the tribe; cf. A. P. Elkin, "Rock Paintings of North-West Australia," *Oceania*, I (December, 1930), 257–79; *idem, Studies in Australian Totemism* ("Oceania Monographs," No. 2 [Sydney, 1933]), pp. 67–73. Grey's caves were found again in June, 1947, by H. Coate; cf. A. P. Elkin, "Grey's Northern Kimberley Cave-Paintings Re-found," *Oceania*, XIX (September, 1948), 1–15. Coate was able to collect some information from the natives in regard to these two caves. The first one seems to be connected with sexual relations and Wondjina (Elkin, "Grey's Northern Kimberley Cave-Paintings Re-found," p. 9); the second, discovered by Grey on March 27, belongs to another mythological tradition, namely, that of Galaru, the Rainbow Serpent (*ibid.*, pp. 10–11). For a comparative study, cf. E. A. Worms, "Contemporary and Prehistoric Rock Paintings in Central and Northern Kimberley," *Anthropos*, L (1955), 546–66; A. P. Elkin, "The Origin and Interpretation of Petroglyphs in South-East Australia," *Oceania*, XX (1949–50), 119–57; A. P. Elkin and C. H. and R. M. Berndt, *Art in Arnhem Land* (Melbourne, 1950); Agnes Schulz, "North-West Australian Rock-Paintings," *Memoirs of the National Museum of Victoria*, No. 20 (Melbourne, 1956), pp. 7–57; Charles P. Mountford, *Art, Myth* and *Symbolism*, in his *Records of the American-Australian Scientific Expedition to Arnhem Land* (hereinafter cited as *"Records"*), Vol. I (Melbourne, 1956), cf. R. M. Berndt, "The Mountford Volume on Aboriginal Art," *Mankind*, V (October, 1958), 249–61; A. P. Elkin, "Art and Meaning: A Review Article," *Oceania*, XXXIII (September, 1961), 54–58; F. D. McCarthy, *The Cave Paintings of Groote Eylandt and Chasm Island*, in Mountford, *Records*, II (Melbourne, 1960), 297–414. Cf. also W. Arndt, "The Interpretation of the Delemere Lightning Paintings and Rock Engravings," *Oceania*, XXXII (March, 1962), 163–77.

morphic Being, the Wondjina. The Wondjinas are associated with sky, rain, the Rainbow Serpent, spirit children,
and fertility. Capell describes them as "superhuman beings
(male or female) whose homes are in caves," who "possess
life-giving powers associated with waters," and who are
related to the Rainbow Serpent, which is considered by
Capell to represent a later religious creation.[52] But the structural continuity of all these mythological figures is also
demonstrated by the etymologies of their names. E. A.
Worms has proved that the terms *wondjina, ungur,* and
ungud are all connected with the widely found Australian
and Tasmanian root *wan-, wun-, win-,* "water." Wondjina
literally means "near the water"; Ungur and Ungud, "belonging to the water."[53]

A. P. Elkin has observed that, among the Ungarinyin,
the name Ungud refers to the mythical time and to the
Rainbow Serpent; but it is also equivalent to Wondjina.[54]
"The Wondjina paintings are therefore efficacious because
they are Ungud, because they were instituted by Ungud,
or in the Ungud time."[55] According to Petri,[56] the Ungarinyin have three names or concepts for the personages
of the primeval times: Ungur, Ungud, and Wondjina. The
aborigines consider Ungur and Ungud to be similar to the
Wondjina; but they are "more boss" than the Wondjina.
It is probable that Ungur refers to the primordial time

[52] A. Capell, "Mythology in Northern Kimberley," pp. 389 ff.,
403.
[53] Worms, "Contemporary and Prehistoric Rock Paintings," pp.
549–50.
[54] Elkin, "Rock Paintings of North-West Australia," pp. 263;
269, n. 8.
[55] *Ibid.,* p. 276.
[56] Petri, *Sterbende Welt,* pp. 102–3.

when Ungud, the Rainbow Serpent, carried out the Creation. The Wondjina are the Heroes and lawgivers[57] who came forth from Ungud and who continued the Creation at the Ungud sites.

Ungud is invisible to all human beings, except for the medicine man. The *bán-man* ("Ungud doctor") not only can see Ungud; he speaks to him. Ungud gives the medicine man his magical powers, which are symbolized in the *kimba*, or quartz crystals. The quartz crystals are believed to have had a celestial origin. Indeed, Ungud, the master and protector of the waters, being the Rainbow Serpent, also extends to the sky. From a certain point of view, one might say that Ungud represents the mythological expression of the effort to unite the opposites, to articulate the polarities in a single paradoxical unity.

Let us add that the Rainbow Serpent[58] is an important

[57] It has been remarked that the figures of the Wondjina give the impression of a skull without jaws (cf. Adam, "Anthromorphe und Darstellungen," p. 22, n. 44). The painted image may resemble a corpse, that is to say, the body of a Hero who transformed himself into a painting at the time of his death, while his spirit descended into a nearby Ungud pool, ready to act when his image is repainted (cf. Elkin, "Grey's Northern Kimberley Cave-Paintings Re-found," p. 12). The caves are often the place for the final disposal of the bones of those who are spiritually related to the nearby water pool (Elkin, "Rock-Paintings of North-West Australia," p. 278).

[58] A. R. Radcliffe-Brown, "The Rainbow-Serpent Myth of Australia," *Journal of the Royal Anthropological Institute*, LVI (1926), 19–26; *idem*, "The Rainbow-Serpent Myth in South-East Australia," *Oceania*, I (1930), 342–47; Ursula McConnel, "The Rainbow-Serpent in North Queensland," *Oceania*, I (1930), 347–49; Elkin, "The Rainbow-Serpent Myth in North-West Australia," *Oceania*, I (1930), 349–52; Ralph Piddington, "The Water-Serpent

mythological figure in many parts of Australia, and almost everywhere it is supposed to convey to medicine men their magical powers in the form of crystals. Thus it appears that *the Creation, the rain, fertility, and the supernatural powers of the medicine men are traced to one and the same source: a primordial Supreme Being of a cosmic structure;* for Ungud belongs concomitantly to the subterranean waters, to earth, and to heaven. The Rainbow Serpent appears *ab initio*, at the very beginning of the world. The Wondjina completed the Creation; but their powers are derived from the Rainbow Serpent, just as the powers of the medicine man originate from him. We have here an exemplary primordial figure. The Rainbow Serpent can be compared with the Mesopotamian Tiamat and other ophidian Beings of the Oriental cosmogonies. But such a comparison is only partially valid, for Ungud, the Rainbow Serpent, was never conquered and displaced by a younger divinity as Taimat was conquered by Marduk. For the Ungarinyin there is perfect continuity between Ungud, the Wondjina, and the individuals who, up to our own day, keep their world alive. Moreover, the medicine men continue to maintain direct personal relations with the Rainbow Serpent.

Reiterating the Creativity of the Dream Time

The religious actuality of Ungud and the Wondjina is demonstrated particularly by their powers as the source of rain and of fertility. In northern Kimberley, if a rock painting is touched by a man from the proper totemic clan, rain will fall and the spirit children will become available

---

in Karadjeri Mythology," *Oceania*, I (1930), 352–54. Cf. also John Loewenstein, "Rainbow and Serpent," *Anthropos*, LVI (1961), 31–40.

for incarnation. Likewise, repainting the animal and vegetal images is said to increase the respective species. "In one part of Northern Kimberley the man who finds a spirit-child, must go to the gallery and touch up the painting of the rainbow-serpent, and even paint a representation of a spirit-child, so that the former will be able to keep up the supply."[59]

These spirit children are pre-existent; while unborn, they sojourn in well-defined sites. "The pre-existent spirits for the most part came into existence during the long-past dream time as a result of some activity of a hero; according to some beliefs, however, they are made from time to time or brought into being by a creative hero whose activity was not confined to the past but is continuous."[60] Among the Ungarinyin, Petri found only the belief that the spirit child is found by the father in a dream; cohabitation is considered merely to be a pleasure.[61] Similar conceptions are attested among many neighboring tribes of the Ungarinyin.[62] And, as is well known, all over central Australia procreation is not directly associated with sexual intercourse.[63]

The "increase" of the animal and vegetal species by re-painting the rock figures is not a magic act but a religious one.[64] The men are *reactivating their contact with the*

[59] Elkin, *The Australian Aborigines*, p. 201; cf. *Oceania*, I, 262.

[60] Elkin, *The Australian Aborigines*, p. 198.

[61] Petri, *Sterbende Welt*, p. 163.

[62] *Ibid.*, p. 170.

[63] Cf. M. F. Ashley-Montagu, *Coming into Being among the Australian Aborigines* (New York, 1938). But see now T. G. H. Strehlow, "La Gémellité de l'âme humaine," *La Tour Saint-Jacques*, No. 11–12 (Paris, 1957), pp. 14–23; *idem*, "Personal Monototem-ism," pp. 730 ff.

[64] Petri, *Sterbende Welt*, pp. 197 ff., 215–16; Elkin, *The Australian Aborigines*, pp. 199 ff.

source of life. Thus the creativity of the Dream Time is again reiterated on earth. The same principle informs the "increase ceremonies" (*intichiuma* or, to use the more general Aranda term, *mbanbiuma*) of the central Australians, so abundantly described by Spencer and Gillen. The ceremonies are carried out at spots associated with the mythical history of the tribe: that is, the sites where the totemic Heroes performed the rituals for the first time. Each actor represents a mythical Ancestor; as a matter of fact, he reincarnates that Ancestor. Each ceremony lasts only a few minutes, and while it is being performed the audience chants a song narrating the mythical episode in process of re-enactment. At the conclusion of each ritual, the old men explain its meaning and the meaning of the decorations and symbols to the newly initiated youth.[65] As Strehlow puts it, the chorus of old men "chant those verses of the traditional song which commemorate the original scene in the life of the ancestor which has been dramatized in the ceremony witnessed by them."[66]

Among the Karadjeri, notes Piddington, the increase ceremonies take place at specific centers, founded during the *bugari* ("dream") time, where the spirits of the species had been left in abundance. Sometimes the performers chant a song associated with the mythical origin of the community.[67]

Thus the increase of a natural species is brought about through a reactivation of the contact with the Dream Time

[65] Spencer and Gillen, *Native Tribes of the Northern Territory of Australia*, pp. 318 ff.

[66] Strehlow, *Aranda Traditions*, pp. 56–57.

[67] Ralph Piddington, "Totemic System of the Karadjeri Tribe," *Oceania*, II, No. 4 (1932), 377–78.

Heroes, and *such a reactivation can be brought about by refreshing the rock paintings (Wondjina), by re-enacting the original creative act,* or *by chanting the myth* in which this episode is narrated.

CHAPTER 3

Initiation Rites
and Secret Cults

Puberty Rites

Ultimately, all Australian religious activities can be considered as so many different but homologous means of re-establishing contact with the Supernatural Beings and of immersing oneself in the sacred time of the "Dreaming." Every religious act—a ritual, the recital of a myth, a secret chant, the making of a sacred instrument, and so on—is only the *repetition* of an event that took place in the beginning of time, in short, an imitation of models revealed to the tribe by Supernatural Beings. On the other hand, every individual is fundamentally a "spiritual" being. His most secret self is a part of that sacred world he is periodically trying to recontact. But he does not know his own real identity: this must be revealed to him through the initiation rites. Thus, one may say that the initiation reinstates the young Australian in his original, spiritual mode of being. As W. Lloyd Warner says with regard to each Murngin male, "the personality before birth is purely spiritual; it becomes completely profane or unspiritual in the earlier period of its life when it is classed socially with the females, gradually becomes more and more ritualized and sacred as the individual grows older and approaches death, and at death once more becomes completely spiritual and sacred."[1]

[1] W. Lloyd Warner, *A Black Civilization: A Study of an Aus-*

The Australian initiation ceremonies accomplish a gradual introduction of the novice into the sacred world.[2] This means, first, that the novice will be separated from the profane world of childhood, where he was under the care and guidance of his mother, and, second, there will be disclosed a sacred history which eventually will bring about the understanding of his own spiritual identity.

Some time before, a "sacred ground" has been prepared, where the men will perform their secret rituals. The sacred ground is arranged differently according to the traditions of each tribe, but it is always related to the mythical events that are to be progressively re-enacted by dances, chants, and pantomimes. In some cases, the sacred ground represents an image of the world as it was made in the beginning, when the world was sanctified by the presence of the Supernatural Beings. Thus, according to R. H. Mathews, the Kamilaroi used to prepare two circular enclosures. The larger, about seventy feet in diameter, had a pole three yards high in the center "with a bunch of emu's feathers tied on the top." In the smaller circle, two young trees were fixed in the ground with their roots in the air. The two circles were connected by a path. "On either side of

tralian Tribe (originally published 1937; rev. ed., 1958; reprint, New York: Harper Torchbooks, 1964), pp. 5–6.

[2] On age-grading ceremonies and other types of initiation, see Eliade, Birth and Rebirth. For more recent bibliographies, see C. Bleeker (ed.), Initiation (Leiden, 1965). For other interpretations of the puberty rites, cf. M. Whiting, R. Kluckhohn, and A. Anthony, "The Functions of Male Initiation Ceremonies at Puberty," in E. E. Maccoby, Theodore Newcomb, and C. Hartley (eds.), Readings in Social Psychology (New York, 1958), pp. 359–70; Edward Norbeck, D. Walker, and M. Cohen, "The Interpretation of Data: Puberty Rites," American Anthropologist, LXIV (1962), 463–85.

the path a number of figures are drawn on the ground or modelled in clay. The largest, which is fifteen feet in height, is that of the Supreme Being, Baiami. A couple represents the mythical Ancestors, and a group of twelve human figures stands for the young men who were with Baiami in his first camp. Other figures represent animals and nests."[3] The novices are not allowed to look at these images, which will be destroyed at the end of the ceremony.

According to Mathews, the "*bora* ground represents Baiame's first camp, the people who were with him while there, and the gifts he presented them with."[4] That is to say, the participants in the ceremony relive the mythical epoch in which the initiation (*bora*) was held for the first time. They reintegrate the sacred time when Baiame was present on earth and founded the mysteries that are now performed. In short, there is a reactualization of Baiame's presence and creative works, and hence a regeneration of the world, for the world is renewed by the reproduction of its exemplary model, Baiame's first camp.[5] As we shall

---

[3] Eliade, *Birth and Rebirth*, p. 5, summarizing R. H. Mathews, "The Bora or Initiation Ceremonies of the Kamilaroi Tribe," *Journal of the Royal Anthropological Institute*, XXIV (1895), 411–27, esp. 414 ff. The plastic figuration of the Supreme Being is rather exceptional; it is to be found only among the Yuin and the Wiradjuri-Kamilaroi. On this problem see W. Koppers, "Zur Frage der bildnerischen Darstellung des Hochgottes." *Ethnologica*, N.F., II (Cologne, 1960), 1–11, esp. 2 ff.

[4] Mathews, "The Bora or Initiation Ceremonies," p. 418. Cf. the description of the clearing in the "men's country," on which the circumcision ceremonies are held, among the Walbiri, in M. G. Meggitt, *Desert People: A Study of the Walbiri Aborigines of Central Australia* (Sydney: Angus and Robertson, 1962), pp. 385 ff. (reissued, Chicago and Toronto, 1965).

[5] Eliade, *Birth and Rebirth*, p. 6.

see, this is true of all Australian initiation ceremonies. Innumerable ritual pantomimes with their related chants are
displayed on such sacred grounds, far from the main camp.
Very few of them are intelligible to the novices. But this
reactualization of the most important episodes of the sacred
history of the tribe renews contact with the sacred world.
The initiation ceremonies are as important for the spiritual
life of the community as they are for the mystical metamorphosis of the novices.

The separation from the mother takes place more or less
dramatically. The least dramatic ritual is found among the
Kurnai, where, as a matter of fact, the entire initiation
ceremony is quite simple. "The mothers sit behind the
novices; the men come forward in single file between the
two groups and so separate them. The instructors raise
the novices into the air several times, the novices stretching
their arms as far as possible toward the sky. . . . They are
then led into the sacred enclosure, where lying on their
backs with their arms crossed on their chests, they are
covered with rugs. From then on they see and hear nothing. After a monotonous song, they fall asleep; later, the
women withdraw."[6] But among other tribes, especially in
the central and northern parts of the continent, the women
not only cry and lament, but also try to resist, at least
symbolically; in some places, they even use spears against
the men who are approaching to take the young boys away.[7]

[6] *Ibid.*, p. 7, summarizing Howitt, *The Native Tribes of South-
East Australia*, pp. 625 ff. Cf. also Eliade, *Birth and Rebirth*, pp.
7–9, for some other examples of initiation among southeastern Australian tribes.

[7] Elkin, *The Australian Aborigines*, p. 179. "All the female relatives grab up spears and spear-throwers and pretend to fight the
men to prevent them from removing the boys" (Warner, *A Black
Civilization*, p. 251).

The age at which the boys begin their initiation varies from six or eight to twelve or even fourteen years. The duration of the ceremonies also varies, from a few months to two or three years. But the most important differences are in the types of bodily operations undergone by the novices. Notwithstanding all these variations, the Australian age-grading ceremonies fall into a pattern. Generally speaking, every puberty initiation series includes the following elements: (*a*) the segregation of the novices in a special isolated camp or in the bush; (*b*) the instruction received from their tutors; (*c*) certain bodily operations; (*d*) the disclosure of ritual objects and the acceptance of novices at some secret ceremonies; (*e*) the final washing, that is, the cleaning off of all traces of the sacred world and the ceremonial return to ordinary life.[8]

As we shall presently see, most of the initiatory rituals and behaviors are informed with the symbolism of death and resurrection (or death and rebirth). As a matter of fact, the novice dies to the profane world of childhood and irresponsible innocence, the world of ignorance, and prepares himself for rebirth as a spiritual being.[9] The mothers and

---

[8] Cf. Eliade, *Birth and Rebirth*, p. 4; Elkin, *The Australian Aborigines*, pp. 179–84; R. M. and C. H. Berndt, *The World of the First Australians*, pp. 136–47. The essential bibliography on Australian initiation is quoted in Eliade, *op. cit.*, pp. 138–44. See especially F. Speiser, "Über Initiationen in Australien und Newguinea," *Verhandlungen der Naturforschenden Gesellschaft in Basel* (1929), pp. 56–258; R. Piddington, "Karadjeri Initiation," *Oceania*, III (1932–33), 46–87; Norman B. Tindale, "Initiation among the Pitjandjara Natives of the Mann and Tomkinson Ranges in South Australia," *Oceania*, VI (1935), 199–224; E. A. Worms, "Initiationsfeiern einiger Küsten- und Binnenlandstämme in Nord-Westaustralien," *Annali Lateranensi*, II (1938), 147–74; Warner, *A Black Civilization*, pp. 114 ff.; Meggitt, *Desert People*, pp. 281–316.

[9] "The mothers and the father's sisters together also represent

the womenfolk, as well as all the initiates, understand this ritual death literally. The mothers are convinced that their boys will be killed or swallowed by mysterious and hostile Supernatural Beings. But they also know that the boys will come back to life again, although not as they were before initiation: *their* children. For this reason they mourn over the novices as the dead are mourned.[10] As for the initiates, their trials and conduct during the seclusion period, and particularly the different bodily operations, continuously emphasize their ritual death. For example, they may be covered with branches or rugs, and they are not permitted to use words, only sounds and signs. The novice "is even carried about on some occasions as though he were helpless. In some tribes he is laid along the top angular space formed by two lines of men crossing their spears, and there he has to lie as though he had been killed by the spears, while the two lines move about, and the women cry."[11]

Even the most simple ritual operation—knocking out one of the incisors—symbolizes the death of the novice at the hands of a Supernatural Being. During the operation the bull-roarer sounds, indicating the presence of the Supernatural Being. Among the Wiradjuri, the novices are told that Daramulun is coming to burn them. But after the tooth evulsion, the instructors point to the bull-roarer and say: "This is Daramulun!" The novices are allowed to touch and whirl the bull-roarer, and they are told the myth of the origin of initiation (Daramulun boasts that during the initiation he kills the boys, cuts them to pieces, burns them,

---

the secular world that the neophyte is leaving, whereas his fathers and his mother's brothers stand for the secret life he is entering" (Meggitt, *Desert People*, p. 293).

[10] Cf. Eliade, *Birth and Rebirth*, pp. 8–9.

[11] Elkin, *The Australian Aborigines*, pp. 180–81.

and then restores them to life, "new beings, but each with a tooth missing."[12]

Symbolic Death

Circumcision, which is probably the most important Australian initiation rite, is the ritual killing par excellence.[13] The performers of the operation incarnate or represent Supernatural, rather demonic, Beings. Among some tribes, the bull-roarers are whirled before the operation and are shown to the novices immediately afterward.[14] The meaning is obvious: the circumcision is effectuated by a representative

[12] Mathews, summarized in Eliade, *Birth and Rebirth*, p. 13. On the tooth evulsion, cf., also R. M. and C. H. Berndt, *The World of the First Australians*, pp. 140–41.

[13] "The Walbiri explicitly equate circumcision with ritual killing" (Meggitt, *Desert People*, p. 294). We do not intend to discuss here the meanings and functions of circumcision among the primitives in general. The psychological "origins" of circumcision are irrelevant for the historian of religions; he is interested only in the religious values and meanings bestowed upon this operation in various cultures and in different times. On circumcision as an initiatory ordeal, see Eliade, *Birth and Rebirth*, pp. 21 ff., 141 ff. Cf. also Ad. E. Jensen, *Beschneidung und Reifezeremonien bei Naturvölkern* (Stuttgart, 1933); F. Speiser, "Über die Beschneidung in der Südsee," *Acta Tropica*, I (1944), 9–29; F. R. Lehmann, "Bemerkungen zu einer neuen Begründung der Beschneidung," *Sociologus*, VII (1957), 57–74; R. M. and C. H. Berndt, *The World of the First Australians*, pp. 143 ff.

[14] See some examples in Eliade, *Birth and Rebirth*, pp. 21–22, 141. On bull-roarers in Australia, cf. O. Zerries, *Das Schwirrholz. Untersuchung über die Verbreitung und Bedeutung des Schwirrens im Kult* (Stuttgart, 1942), pp. 84–125. Speiser considers the Australian bull-roarer to be of Melanesian origin; see "Kulturgeschichtliche Betrachtungen über die Initiationen in der Südsee," *Bulletin der Schweizerischen Gesellschaft für Anthropologie und Ethnalogie*, XXII (1945–46), 28–61, esp. 50 ff.

of the Supernatural Beings whose "voice" is heard in the sound of the bull-roarer. But the novice is also instructed about the actual source of the Supernatural Being's "voice." In other cases, the killing of the initiate is represented as a swallowing by a gigantic monstrous Being, usually a Snake. But the meaning of circumcision can change when the initiation ceremony is integrated into a new cult. Thus, in western Arnhem Land, today's novices are "identified with those who were born, in the beginning, to the Djanggawul Sisters. A boy who has just had his foreskin cut off is said to have emerged from his Mother, here meaning Djanggawul."[15]

Other less important operations are depilation of body or facial hair, a ritual found mostly among the noncircumcising tribes,[16] and cicatrization, in which Elkin deciphers a "death" significance.[17] In a number of tribes the initiate undergoes a second operation, the subincision, some time after the circumcision. The interval between the two operations varies, from five or six weeks among the Aranda to two or three years among the Karadjeri. The original religious meaning of subincision is still somewhat unclear.[18]

[15] R. M. and C. H. Berndt, *The World of the First Australians,* p. 145.

[16] See, *inter alia, ibid.,* p. 142.

[17] Elkin, *The Australian Aborigines,* pp. 173, 182.

[18] See Eliade, *Birth and Rebirth,* pp. 25 ff., and the bibliographies quoted on pp. 142 ff. Cf. especially H. Basedow, "Subincision and Kindred Rites of the Australian Aboriginal," *Journal of the Royal Anthropological Institute,* LVIII (1927), 123–56; Ashley-Montagu, *Coming into Being among the Australian Aborigines,* pp. 302 ff.; Bruno Bettelheim, *Symbolic Wounds* (1st ed.; Glencoe, Ill., 1954), pp. 173 ff.; J. Winthuis, *Das Zweigeschelchterwesen* (Leipzig, 1928), pp. 29 ff.; H. Baumann, *Das doppelte Geschlecht. Ethnologische Studien zur Bisexualität in Ritus und Mythos* (Berlin,

In some cases, the idea of bisexuality is emphatically stressed, for example, among the Pitta-Pitta and the Boubia of northwest central Queensland, who assimilate the sub-incision wound to the vulva.[19] But the primary purpose of the operation seems to be obtaining fresh blood for use in religious ceremonies. It is probable that even in this case the original model was the menstrual flow. As a matter of fact, two purposes can be served by imitating the "women's mysteries." Just as the women get rid of "bad blood" by menstruation, the initiate can expel his mother's blood by laceration of the subincision wound.[20] Second, the laceration amply provides the blood needed for the ceremonies. For, almost everywhere in Australia, at a certain moment during the initiation a blood rite is performed.

It consists of anointing the newly initiated with arm-blood from the older men, or else giving them some of this to drink. The older men also anoint themselves or each other and drink blood. This blood is sacred; there is a secret name for it, and it is usually associated with some mythical hero's act. It gives life, strength and courage and so fits the candidates for the revelations which are to be made. At the same time it unites them to the elders of whose blood they have partaken; indeed, it does more; it unites them to the initiation heroes, for the

---

1955), pp. 313 ff.; R. M. and C. H. Berndt, *The World of the First Australians*, pp. 145–46.

[19] W. E. Roth, *Ethnological Studies among the North-West-Central Queensland Aborigines* (Brisbane and London, 1897), p. 180. Cf. also other examples quoted in Eliade, *Birth and Rebirth*, p. 26.

[20] This idea is current in New Guinea. A Kuman explained to John Nilles: "This is done to release the bad blood accumulated since he was in his mother's womb, his inheritance from the woman" (quoted in Eliade, *Birth and Rebirth*, p. 27.

blood taken under such conditions is the hero's or ancestor's life, and so to drink it, brings the initiated into the mythical world. A special song must be chanted while this blood is being drawn, and this changes it—consecrates it, as we would say, and gives it sacramental efficacy.[21]

Ronald and Catherine Berndt think that anointing the novice with blood emphasizes anew his ritual death. (*The World of the First Australians*, p. 141). In some cases, red ochre is substituted for blood.

The most important concluding rituals are the fire ceremony and the washing. The fire ceremonies are universally diffused; according to Elkin they may leave the greatest impression on the initiates. The novices are "roasted" near the fire, or they stare at the flames until they are almost dazed, or burning coals are thrown on them, or they are dropped onto thickly smoking fire, and so on.[22] These fire ceremonies have both an initiatory and a purificatory function. On the one hand, the ritual "roasting" is supposed to achieve a sort of mysterious transmutation of the novice. The exemplary model of such transmutations is the "mastery over fire" displayed by shamans and medicine men in so many archaic and traditional cultures.[23] From a certain point of view, one can say that the fire ceremonies proclaim in a very concrete and dramatic way the results of the initiation: the novice shows his spiritual transformation.

[21] Elkin, *The Australian Aborigines*, p. 183; cf. also pp. 173–74; Eliade, *Birth and Rebirth*, pp. 26 ff.

[22] Elkin, *The Australian Aborigines*, p. 183. On ritual "roasting" of the novices, see Eliade, *Birth and Rebirth*, p. 7 and n. 13 (bibliography); Bettelheim, *Symbolic Wounds*, pp. 180 ff.

[23] Cf. Eliade, *Shamanism*, pp. 474 ff.; *idem, The Forge and the Crucible* (New York: Harper, 1962), pp. 79 ff.

The "natural condition" (fear of fire, the inevitable combustion of that which is put in contact with burning coals, etc.) now gives place to a "spiritual" mode of being.

Moreover, Elkin points out that the fire ceremony is usually the final rite in the initiation series (*The Australian Aborigines*, p. 185). Thus purified, the newly initiated may safely come back to the secular world. The washing has the same purpose: to annihilate all traces of the sacred world (the blood used in decoration, etc.) before coming in contact with the uninitiated. "Preparations are made by the women for the return which is carried out ceremonially. The newly initiated is welcomed as one returned from the dead" (*ibid.*).

Nevertheless, the essential element of initiation is not to be found among the bodily operations;[24] it is rather the novice's experiences and instruction while living away from the main camp. The seclusion in the bush in itself constitutes an experience of ritual death. The novice is dying to the profane world of childhood. He is gradually introduced to the sacred history of the tribe and is permitted to witness, at least in part, its pantomimes and ceremonial dances. It seems as if no *real* change in the human mode of being can be achieved without "dying" to the previous condition. The passage from a "natural" to a "spiritual" mode of being cannot take place except through a ritual death followed

[24] "I have . . . mentioned the physical operations because many white folk imagine that the operation is initiation and that, having been present at a circumcision or tooth-knocking rite they really understand Aboriginal secrets. The bodily operations, however, are not the important and essential element of initiation . . . They can . . . be omitted if circumstances render such a step necessary, without endangering the real purpose and effect of initiation" (Elkin, *The Australian Aborigines*, p. 172).

by a resurrection or a new birth. Death is the paradigmatic expression of the end of a mode of being. Obviously, this is not an exclusive particularity of the Australian religions. Initiation as a symbolic death and resurrection is widely known in the history of religions. But what seems to be characteristic of the Australian form is, on the one hand, the fact that the entire religious life is grounded in the experiences and revelations of the age-grading ceremonies and, on the other hand, the fact that a great number of liturgical cycles are usually performed on the occasion of such initiations.

Initiation and Anamnesis

But the ritual death is only a preliminary condition for the novice's introduction to the sacred history of the tribe. In learning the myths and the rituals, the novice also learns about his personal relations with, and responsibilities toward, the actors of that sacred history. It is a very complex type of "learning," related to all levels and dimensions of human existence. As Ronald and Catherine Berndt put it:

Although initiation involves training for life, it is training for a special kind of life. They learn more about their place in the local scheme of things, man in relation to man; man in relation to the natural environment; and man in relation to his gods. The fundamentals of these are assumed to have been learnt before, and only practice will make perfect. But the kind of knowledge which is transmitted through the initiation rituals is the inherited and accumulated store of knowledge handed down from the past—reinterpreted, it is true, to conform with current conditions, but kept as far as possible in the mould of the past.[25]

[25] R. M. and C. H. Berndt, *The World of the First Australians*, p. 182.

Of course, the "past" is so religiously valuable because it is related to the sacred history of the tribe, that is, to the "Dreaming," the mythical time. Through initiation, the novice discovers that the world has a hidden meaning that cannot be grasped by ordinary intellectual operations but must be revealed and explained by the older men. This is for the simple reason that the meaning of the world, of life, and of human existence is finally the result, not of a "natural" process, but of a series of mythical events—in sum, of a sacred history. And one of the most moving experiences of initiation occurs when the novice becomes wholly conscious of his personal relations with the sacred history of the tribe. As we have already pointed out,[26] in some cases the initiation is equivalent to an anamnesis. The neophyte discovers and assumes his real identity, not in the "natural," immediate world in which he had moved before his initiation, but in a "spiritual" universe which first and gloriously emerged in the mythical time of the beginnings and never completely vanished thereafter.

This is particularly evident among the Aranda. According to T. G. H. Strehlow, after the preliminary rites (isolation of the novice, circumcision, subincision), at the end of the probation period, the elders decide to make the new initiate the owner of his personal *tjurunga*.[27] The neophyte is taken to the storehouse of the sacred objects. His father or his father's brother explains to him the significance of

[26] See Chapter 2, p. 58.

[27] On the mythology and rituals of *tjurungas* see Spencer, *Native Tribes of the Northern Territory of Australia*, pp. 143 ff.; Spencer and Gillen, *The Northern Tribes of Central Australia*, pp. 257 ff.; *idem*, *The Arunta*, I, 99 ff.; Strehlow, *Aranda Traditions*, pp. 54 ff., 85–86, etc. Cf. also L. Adams, "Anthropomorphe Darstellungen auf australischen Ritualgeräten," *Anthropos*, LIII (1958), 1–50.

the various physical objects of the sacred site. "A large party of other men belonging to the totemic clan on whose territory the cave is situated accompany the young man. There is one correct trail, and one only, by which the ceremonial site may be approached. It is firmly fixed by tradition for every ancient storehouse."[28] In the mountainous regions, the *tjurungas* are deposited in caves. In northern Aranda territory, they are usually placed on platforms erected among the branches of a mulga tree. When approaching the sacred site the men lay down their weapons and start talking in whispers or using sign language. Finally they sit down near the mulga tree, while the leader climbs the platform and brings down the bundles of *tjurungas*. He passes them to the old men, and as each *tjurunga* is being handed around, the verse "belonging" to it is chanted. Everyone presses the *tjurunga* to his body. When it is handed to the novice, the elders explain its marks and ornaments, and also the mythical event evoked by the chant. Eventually the *tjurungas* are replaced on the platform in their bundles.

The party returns to the two clusters of stones in the clay hollow a few yards away. The old leader lifts up the rough stone from the top of one heap, revealing a round, smooth, red-ochred stone underneath. The father of the young initiate then takes the hand of his son, leads him to the cluster, and places the smooth round stone into his hands. Having obtained the permission of the other old men present, he tells his son: "This is your own body from which you have been re-born. It is the true body of the great Tjenterama, the chief of the Ilbalintja storehouse. The stones which cover him are the bodies of the bandicootmen who once lived at the Ilbalintja Soak. You

[28] Strehlow, *Aranda Traditions*, p. 114.

are the great Tjenterama himself, today you are learning the truth for the first time. From now on you are the chief of Ilbalintja: all its sacred *tjurungas* are entrusted to your safe keeping. Protect them, guard the home of your fathers, honour the traditions of your people. We still have many things to tell you. More verses, greater and more secret ceremonies will be made known to you than to any of your mates. They are all your own heritage: we have only kept them in trust for you. Now we are getting old, and we pass them on to you since you are the true chief reincarnate. Keep them secret until you are growing old and weak; and then, if no other young men of the bandicoot totem are living, pass them on to other tried men from our clan who may keep alive the traditions of our forefathers until another chief be born."[29]

The initiate is taught by his father and the old men the chant containing the name of Tjenterama. This name, which henceforth will be his real name, must not be pronounced in the presence of women, children, or foreigners. The small stone is greased and red ochred and replaced in its hole, hidden under the other stones as before. In the evening the party returns home, and a sacred ceremony is held in honor of the newly made chief of Ilbalintja. For the rest of his life, no one is allowed to perform that ceremony again except in the presence and with the permission of the chief.[30]

Sometimes the initiate is not taken to the sacred site. Two or more old men bring the *tjurunga*, and the father shows it to his son. "Young man, see this object. This is your own body. This is the tjilpa ancestor who you were when you used to wander about in your previous existence. Then you

[29] *Ibid.*, pp. 117–18.   [30] *Ibid.*, pp. 118 ff.

sank down to rest in the sacred cave nearby. This is your own *tjurunga*. Keep close watch over it."[31]

The initiate receives his *tjurunga* when he is twenty-five years old. By the time he is thirty-five to forty years old, he knows all the chants and the ritual secrets.[32] For a novice is not taught all the secrets at his first initiation. "He continues to learn about sacred ritual and myth, and so on, all through his life, and he may be middle-aged or relatively old before the final revelations are made to him. Initiation merely opens the door to the secret–sacred and esoteric life of the men of his community. The actual process may go on for a long time, in a series of stages. For instance, he may be able to see certain objects but not yet handle them, or witness certain rites but not participate in them."[33]

Arnhem Land's Secret Cults

A progressive initiation is characteristic of most Australian religions. As a result, there are several classes of initiates, although the phenomenon of the male "secret society" is not yet clearly articulated. In Australia the progressive initiation assures that in due time every novice will obtain all the knowledge he is entitled to receive. But the main reason for gradually introducing the young men into the tribal secret tradition is the fact that the entire community needs periodically, for its own religious equilibrium, a recapture of the sacred time of the beginnings.

Many characteristic examples of secret ceremonies that pursue concomitantly the initiation of youth and the re-

---

[31] *Ibid.*, p. 119.   [32] *Ibid.*, p. 122.
[33] R. M. and C. H. Berndt, *The World of the First Australians,* p. 138.

newal of life by a re-enactment of the sacred history are to be found in Arnhem Land. Such ceremonies celebrate the mysteries of Fertility Mothers and of a mythical Serpent. These secret cults are a relatively recent discovery of Australian ethnology. The first important fieldwork was done by Warner in 1927–29, followed twenty years later by the work of Ronald Berndt.[34] The cults spread rather rapidly in the last forty or fifty years and influenced one another or even coalesced. Thus we have today mostly syncretistic secret fertility cults, although their original form is still recognizable. Among the most widespread ones are the ritual sequences related to the Wauwalak (Wawalag, Wagilag, Wawilak) Sisters and a female and male (Berndt) or a bisexual (Warner) python, Yurlunggur. Their myths underlie three ritual complexes. The first, *djunggawon* (*djungguan*), is an age-grading ceremony; the second, *gunabibi* (Warner) or Kunapipi (Berndt), is primarily a secret fertility cult; the third, *ngurlmak*—in the opinion of Ronald and Catherine Berndt the "most important of the three"—is essentially "revelatory in character."[35]

As a matter of fact, each of these ritual sequences constitutes an initiation ceremony, in the sense that in every one of them a certain number of young men are for the first time introduced to specific secrets of the cult. What characterizes all of them, as well as all other esoteric mysteries of Arnhem Land, is the dominant role played by female Primordial Beings and the importance of sexual

[34] Warner, *A Black Civilization;* Ronald M. Berndt, *Kunapipi* (Melbourne: F. W. Cheshire, 1951); see also W. S. Chaseling, *Yulengor, Nomads of Arnhem Land* (London, 1957).

[35] R. M. and C. H. Berndt, *The World of the First Australians,* p. 240.

and fertility rites and symbols. As we shall presently see, their myths and rituals refer continuously to the religious values of menstrual and afterbirth blood, semen, copulation, fecundity, and birth. The meaning of this apparently recent innovation in comparison with the central and southeastern Australian pattern will retain us later on.

Each of the three ritual sequences illustrates certain portions of a fundamental myth, but the main mythological theme underlies every ceremony in part. The principal personages are the two Wauwalak Sisters and a mythical Snake. Their adventures are related in a cycle of songs which are chanted on the sacred ground during the ceremonies.[36] The myth narrates how the Sisters came into northern Arnhem Land from farther south. Before leaving, the elder Sister had incestuous relations with a member of her clan and was thus pregnant during the journey. She is called "with child," while her younger Sister is called "without child" (Berndt, *Kunapipi*, p. 20). As they walked they caught some animals for their supper, declaring that these animals would become sacred later on and thus play a role in the ceremonies. Then they rested awhile, and the elder Sister gave birth to a girl. When the Mother was able to travel, they went in the direction of the sacred well Muruwul. There they made fire and wanted to cook, but the animals jumped from the fire into the well. The plants which were also in the bag ran away too. They knew that since one of the Sisters was impure because of her afterbirth blood, they ought not to go near the well, in which snakes, including Yurlunggur (Julunggul), lived. Indeed, attracted by the smell of blood, Yurlunggur lifted her head

[36] Some of the sacred songs are published by R. M. Berndt, *Kunapipi*, pp. 85–132.

from the well and spouted water. The Sisters saw the clouds and built a hut to escape the rain. The following night Yurlunggur sent lightning and emerged from the well, crawling toward the hut. The younger Sister tried to keep the snake away by dancing, and her dances are re-enacted in the Kunapipi ceremonies. Finally, the Sisters took refuge in the hut, but Yurlunggur followed them and swallowed both of them and the child. Yurlunggur then returned to the Muruwul well where she met her husband and then boasted to the other snakes that she had swallowed the Wauwalak Sisters. Their loud and sinister noise is imitated during the ceremonies by whirling bull-roarers.

There are different versions of the last part of the myth. One of them is the following: "After the swallowing, the female Julunggul returned to Muruwul; there she vomited the Waukalak and child, who were revivified by the bites of the ants, but were eventually re-swallowed. The Wauwalak spirits are still at the sacred well; 'we can't see them, although they can see us, for now they belong to Julunggul.' When they see human beings coming to this site, the Julunggul swallows them again in their spirit form."[37]

We shall come back to the most relevant episodes of the myth while describing the rituals that depend on them. We shall also discuss the religious structure of the Snake, taking into consideration not only the Wauwalak theme but other Australian mythicoritual systems as well. For the moment, we may point out the complex symbolism of Yurlunggur. To start with, the sex of the Snake is not clear. Warner asserts that there is only one Snake, a male one,[38] while

[37] *Ibid.*, p. 31. See also the myth of Waukalak women in Warner, *A Black Civilization*, pp. 240–49.

[38] See, e.g., Warner, *A Black Civilization*, pp. 238–40, 242 ff., etc.

Ronald Berndt thinks that there are two Snakes, a male and a female. Berndt quotes the natives' interpretation, that Yurlunggur entering into the hut is "like a penis going into a vagina."[39] On the other hand, the act of swallowing seems to have a feminine symbolism, for after swallowing the Sisters, Yurlunggur becomes pregnant. Most probably these variations and apparent contradictions point to an original bisexuality of the Snake. And we shall see that the bisexuality is only one, though the most impressive, expression of the "divine totality" (ideally, a *coincidentia opositorum*).

Djunggawon

The first ritual sequence, the age-grading *djunggawon*, begins with the call of the sacred trumpet (*yurlunggur*). The novices are told by their fathers and other men, "The Great Father Snake smells your foreskin. He is calling for it" (Warner, *A Black Civilization*, p. 251). After a series of preliminaries (journey of the young boys to visit the various relatives and clans and invite them to the coming ceremony, etc.) the novices are decorated and painted and taken to the sacred ground. There is a series of dances around a sacred pole accompanied by the chant "A-wa!— a-wa!" which is the sound of falling rain. "They do that because those two old women did that when they tried to stop the rain" (p. 256). Ordinarily older women do the dancing and the wailing, and in the native interpretation

---

For Warner, "Muit or Yurlunggur is man and woman, but he is thought of as male" (p. 373).

[39] R. M. Berndt, *Kunapipi*, p. 25. Warner writes that "the circumcised penis has the mark of the snake upon it because the python has taken the foreskin and by the operation the blood has been let for the Great Father" (p. 126).

they are "all the same" as the Wauwalak Sisters. Afterward, the older men sing of Yurlunggur and his well, and the *yurlunggur* trumpet is blown over the uncircumcised novices. The native interpretation of this ritual is: "Yurlunggur crawled right into the camp with the women and their children. He swallowed them" (p. 261).[40]

While other songs are chanted and pantomimes are enacted that refer to different incidents of the myth (movements of Yurlunggur, lightning, black rain clouds, etc.), the men cut their arms, and the blood is collected into a paper-bark basin. The dancers paint themselves with this sacrificial blood, considered to be the menses of the Wauwalak Sisters. Warner was told during a ceremony:

That blood we put all over those men is all the same as the blood that come from that old woman's vagina. It isn't the blood of those men any more because it has been sung over and made strong. The hole in the man's arm isn't that hole any more. It is all the same as the vagina of that old woman that had blood coming out of it. This is the blood that snake smelled when he was in the Mirrirmina well. . . . When a man has got blood on him (is ceremonially decorated with it), he is all the same as those two old women when they had blood. All the animals ran away and they couldn't cook them [p. 268].

The following day represents the climax of the ceremony. The dancers are painted with human blood. The boys who are to be circumcised are also painted, but "blood is never used because it is magically too powerful for an uncircumcised boy" (p. 272). The novices are shown the animal dances, and the older men explain their meaning.

---

[40] The version recorded by Warner speaks of two Sisters and their children; cf. pp. 240 ff.

They are also shown the sacred trumpet, *yurlunggur.* "Each initiate is asked to try to blow the trumpet. Then the old men command all of them to 'respect their fathers and mothers,' 'never to tell lies,' 'not to run after women who do not belong to them,' 'not to divulge any of the secrets of the men to the women, men who belong to a lower division of the association, or uninitiated boys,' and all in all to live up to the tribal code" (p. 274). Eventually the young men are circumcised. Then their wounds are steamed over a fire while they are instructed: "You must not use obscene language. You must never tell a lie. You must not commit adultery, etc." (p. 278). Finally the ceremonial trumpet is buried at night in the mud of the totemic well, so that the women will not see it when they approach the site (p. 281).

Though the main purpose of *djunggawon* is the circumcision of young men, the ceremony comprises a great number of rituals restricted exclusively to the already initiated adults. In other words, the age-grading ceremony is integrated into the celebration of certain episodes of the sacred history. Only the previously circumcised young man can be initiated in the Kunapipi secret cult. The reason seems evident, for the principal aim of the cult is universal fertility.

Kunapipi and Ngurlmak

The Kunapipi ritual is usually held in the dry season when food is abundant, in other words, when people are reaping the benefits of previous ceremonies. The ritual sequence may last from two weeks to several months. Messengers are sent out to inform members of neighboring groups. The ritual ground is prepared in the bush, and a bull-roarer is made and anointed with blood. "Some time afterward the first rites take place in the main camp. Men sing the 'outside' or camp version of the Wawalag and Kunapipi songs, while the women dance: non-sacred *garma* or clan songs are also sung. This continues for some weeks."[41] Finally, one evening the bull-roarer is twirled and the voice of Yurlunggur is heard. The Kunapipi leader and all the women call out in answer, just as the Wauwalak Sisters cried when Yurlunggur approached them. The young boys, smeared with red ochre, are taken from the main camp to meet the Snake. In fact, they are an offering to Yurlunggur, and the Snake swallows them. Thus propitiated, Yurlunggur returns to the sacred ground, which symbolizes the Muruwul well.[42] The women lament over the initiates as if they are dead.[43] On the sacred ground,

[41] R. M. and C. H. Berndt, *The World of the First Australians*, p. 241.

[42] The sacred ground itself, shaped in the form of a triangle, is Yurlunggur's body, and the hole at its apex represents the well Muruwul; cf. *ibid.*, p. 241.

[43] In some versions, the boys are not swallowed by Yurlunggur but by another snake, Lu'ningu, who, according to the myth, having seen Yurlunggur swallow and then disgorge the two Sisters, wanted to imitate him. He want wandering about the country, swallowing young men, but when he disgorged them they were dead and sometimes reduced to skeletons. In revenge, men killed him, and later they raised a monument representing him—the two posts called *jelmalandji* (R. M. Berndt, *Kunapipi*, pp. 35 ff.). In the ritual, Berndt writes, the young novices "leaving the main camp for the sacred ground are said to be swallowed by Lu'ningu, just as he swallowed the young men in the Dreaming Era" (p. 37). But the two Snakes—Yurlunggur and Lu'ninga—are confused, for on their return to the main camp, the men tell the women: "All the young boys have gone today; Julunggul has swallowed them up" (p. 41). Cf. also Eliade, *Birth and Rebirth*, pp. 49 and 149 (n. 28).

singing and dancing continue through the night. The dances commemorate the animals that the Sisters tried to cook but that escaped from the fire into Yurlunggur's well.

Dances, pantomimes, and songs go on for some weeks, until a large crescent-shaped trench (*ganala*)—symbolizing the uterus—is dug. At some time the novices are placed in the *ganala* and covered with bark. Two large *jelmalandji* emblems are erected beside the *ganala*, and after the bark sheets are removed the boys are told to look at Yurlunggur emerging from the sacred well. After further dances, firebrands representing the lightning sent by Yurlunggur are thrown over the *ganala* where the novices are crouched. The dancers re-enact the swallowing of the Wauwalak Sisters. According to Ronald Berndt, "the actual swallowing, said to mean coitus, may also symbolize the 'return of the Wauwalak to the uterus of their Mother,' as in the conventional interpretation of Kunapipi mythology. The vomiting of the Wauwalak with their revivification and reswallowing, and their subsequent swallowing in spirit form, extends the symbolism and may be compared with the comings and goings (birth and rebirth) of the totemites to and from the Mother's uterus."[44]

Continuing the ritual, the men open their arm veins and sprinkle blood on one another and into the trench: this is the blood of the Sisters. Finally they dance around the trench, filling it with sand and earth. The main ceremony is almost completed. The final rituals are the ceremonial exchange of wives and the return of the initiates to the ordinary camp. "Ritual licence, widely known as the *gur-*

[44] R. M. Berndt, *Kunapipi*, pp. 31–32. The symbolic *regressus ad uterum* is a well-known motif in many types of initiations; cf. *inter alia*, Eliade, *Birth and Rebirth*, pp. 51 ff.

angara, is an integral part of the Kunapipi. It is said to establish goodwill, to cement the bonds of friendship, bringing members of different groups closer together. Moreover, it draws women further into the sacred scheme of the Kunapipi, and symbolizes fertility, which is the main aim of the ritual."[45] The following morning two forked posts, with a thick connecting pole between them, are set up. The pole is covered with branches, and the freshly initiated boys are placed under them, holding on to the pole with their hands. They are, that is, in the womb, and they will emerge reborn—"their spirit comes out new."[46]

The third ritual, the *ngurlmak,* represents a rather recent addition to the Wauwalak mythological cycle; it was adapted from the Alligator River region. For our purpose *ngurlmak* is important because it re-emphasizes the fertility elements and the bisexual symbolism already present in the first two cults. The myths, as usual, are varied and confused. One of them tells how the Mother came from the islands and, in moving about, left spirit children to become the ancestors of the different tribes.[47] Another myth narrates how a girl was killed by her fiancé, a python with whom she refused to sleep. The python (sometimes a male Rainbow Serpent) made a hollow log, an *ubar,* into which

[45] R. M. and C. H. Berndt, *The World of the First Australians,* pp. 242–43.

[46] R. M. Berndt, *Kunapipi,* p. 53. See also the description of a *gunabibi* ceremony in Warner, *A Black Civilization,* pp. 280–301. Warner considers this ritual constellation an age-grading ceremony.

[47] Elkin, *The Australian Aborigines,* p. 226; R. M. and C. H. Berndt, *The World of the First Australians,* p. 210. "In one version she tried to circumcise the children she had made. At first she was unsuccessful and the children died: in those areas people do not practice circumcision today. But at last she succeeded, and the children survived: in these places, therefore, people continue to circumcise" (*ibid.*).

he entered. Eventually the girl put in her hand and was "bitten" and killed. The *ubar* is one of the most sacred objects, and plays the central role in the *ngurlmak* initiation. During the ceremony, the novice is symbolically "killed" by the Snake. He places his hand in the *ubar*, where it is touched by a *maraiin* stone, representing the Serpent's head. But the symbolism of the *ubar* is still more complex. Among some tribes (e.g., the Gunwinggu) it represents the uterus of the Mother, but it can also be identified with the Rainbow Serpent. Among the Maung at Goulburn Island, the *ubar* is still the womb of the Mother, but it is also the genital organ of the male Rainbow Snake.[48] The hollow log is beaten continuously during the ceremony, and this resonant sound signifies the Mother's voice calling men to the sacred ground. ("In some versions, this ground, the mother's womb, and the ritual is one of rebirth."[49]) In the second part of the ceremony a whistling summons the Rainbow Snake. The Serpent moves, arches his body, and ascends to the sky. "He is the harbinger of rain, rejuvenator of the earth: he is the instrument through which the rebirth of nature is achieved, with the help of the Mother."[50]

The Ancestress and the Snake

All these ceremonies, but especially the last two, are connected with the mystery of maintaining life and fertility

[48] R. M. and C. H. Berndt, *The World of the First Australians*, p. 211. In Goulburn Island, the *ubar* is said to have belonged in the beginning only to women (R. M. and C. H. Berndt , *Sexual Behaviour in Western Arnhem Land* [New York, 1951], p. 122). On this motif, cf. below, pp. 121 ff.

[49] Elkin, *The Australian Aborigines*, p. 226.

[50] R. M. and C. H. Berndt, *The World of the First Australians*, p. 234.

on earth. In the tropical regions of Arnhem Land, life and fertility depend primarily on having the proper amount of rain. For this reason the ritual scenarios of the Ancestresses and of the Rainbow Serpent have been brought together. Most probably, this conjunction is a recent phenomenon, for the Rainbow Serpent is found almost all over the continent, while the cults of the Primordial Mothers are exclusive to Arnhem Land and are known to have been imported from Melanesia.[51] Nevertheless, the convergence of the two systems is most relevant for an understanding of Australian religions. Though limited to the northern part of the continent, such fertility cults disclose a pan-Australian pattern. As everywhere else in Australia, the cult of the Ancestress reiterates a primordial drama. The rituals assure the continuation of the cosmic life and at the same time introduce the initiates to a sacred history that ultimately reveals the meaning of their lives.

Incidentally, the most striking parallel to the Australian ritual re-enactment of the "Creation" is to be found in post-Vedic India. The brahmanic sacrifice repeats what was done in the beginning, at the moment of Creation, and it is only because of the strict and uninterrupted performance of the sacrifice that the world continues and periodically renews itself. Moreover, it is only by identifying himself with the sacrifice that man can conquer death. Likewise, as we have abundantly seen, the Australian religious system consists in the repetition of the paradigmatic acts performed by Supernatural Beings in the Dream Time. It is by this

---

[51] Cf. A. P. Elkin, Preface to R. M. Berndt, *Kunapipi*, p. xxii; Elkin, *The Australian Aborigines*, p. 229; Wilhelm Schmidt, "Mythologie und Religion in Nord Australien," *Anthropos*, XLVIII (1953), 898–924.

continuous imitation of divine models that the Australian keeps his world alive and fertile, understands his proper mode of being, and finally conquers a "spiritual" post existence. Thus, structurally, there is no solution of continuity between the Australian and brahmanic ritual ideologies. This continuity has to be kept in mind when one tries to evaluate the "style" of Australian spiritual creations.

It is interesting to know how the aborigines judge the sacred history they so faithfully relive and re-enact. For the Murngin, for example, the beginning of that fateful drama is related to a primordial sin. If the Wauwalak Sisters " 'hadn't done wrong in their own country and copulated with Dua Wongar men [an incestuous act] and then come down to the Liaalaomir country and menstruated and made that snake wild [angry],' this cycle would never have occurred. 'Everyone and all the plants and animals would have walked about by themselves.' There would have been no copulation between the sexes and no children and no change. 'After they had done this wrong they made it the law for everyone.' "[52] In other words, without that "original sin," the world, life, and human existence would not have been as they are today.

But, on the other hand, the Wauwalak Sisters tried to repent by teaching men the rituals in which the episodes of the primordial drama are continuously re-enacted. Through these rituals, man is purified, and nature is aided in the keeping of its seasonal rhythms. "These ceremonies are designed to aid nature, or possibly it would be better to say to restrain man from preventing by his unclean actions the coming of the dry season of plentitude" (Warner, *A*

[52] Warner, *A Black Civilization*, p. 375.

Black Civilization, p. 376). The world as it is now, man's specific mode of being, *and* "religion"—all this is the result of a primeval sin of the mythical Ancestress. (Let us recall that this is a well-known pattern: even for Judaeo-Christianity, "religion" is the consequence of the Ancestor's fall.) Ultimately, this means that the world and human existence must be accepted as they are because they represent the result of a divine drama. Moreover the authors of the catastrophe taught man how to live in a "fallen" world, and especially instructed him how to avoid aggravating the situation.

Fundamentally, the role of the Ancestresses is ambivalent: they initiated man into their sacred mysteries, but these mysteries are the consequence of their sins. This ambivalence opened the way to countless identifications, in the first place the identification of the Ancestress with the Snake. Kunapipi, which means "Old Woman," "Our Mother," is also one of the names of the Snake who swallowed the Wauwalak Sisters.[53] In the Oenpelli area, "Kunapipi is sometimes identified with Ngaljod, the Rainbow: she is a woman, 'our Mother,' but also a snake, and she may take other shapes too."[54] In the Alligator River region in western Arnhem Land, "our mother from earliest times" becomes identified with the female Rainbow Serpent.[55] The coalescence of the two symbols is even more clearly expressed in the Kunapipi cult, where the subincised penis represents the Snake and the incision itself the womb of the

[53] R. M. Berndt, *Kunapipi,* p. 16.
[54] R. M. and C. H. Berndt, *The World of the First Australians,* p. 245.
[55] Elkin, *The Australian Aborigines,* p. 226.

Mother.[56] As we have already seen, the sexual symbolism of the *ubar* includes both the Mother and the bisexual Snake.

The Rainbow Serpent

These multiple confusions and identifications may reflect historical contact between, and coalescence of, different cults.[57] But, on the other hand, the ambivalence of the Ancestress corresponds to a richer and even more complex ambivalence of the Snake. We have here a characteristic religious phenomenon: a Supreme Being becomes a "totality" by integrating a series of polar and even contradictory attributes and activities. Such a process is encouraged and facilitated by the fundamental religious dialectics of the *coincidentia oppositorum*, which we have studied in many of our previous works.[58] The religious ambivalence of the Snake is illustrated on several levels of reference. We have already said something concerning the sexual ambivalence of Yurlunggur (see p. 103). Stanner's informers described the Rainbow Serpent, Angamunggi, "in terms of the familiar All-Father imagery: as the pri-

[56] R. M. Berndt, *Kunapipi*, p. 16.

[57] See, e.g., J. de Leeuwe, "Male Right and Female Right among the Autochtons of Arnhem Land," *Acta Ethnographica*, XIII (Budapest, 1964), 313–48; XIV (1965), 303–48. The author thinks that the myths and rituals of Arnhem Land point to an archaic gynecocracy of diggers and gatherers which was overthrown later on by the males.

[58] See, e.g., M. Eliade, *Patterns in Comparative Religion* (New York and London, 1958), pp. 415 ff.; *idem, Yoga: Immortality and Freedom* (New York and London, 1958), pp. 244 ff., 267 ff., etc.; *idem, Mephistopheles and the Androgyne* (New York and London, 1966), pp. 78 ff.

meval father of men, the giver of life, the maker of spirit children, and the guardian and protector of life"—but "they suggested that he had a womb."[59] In the Roper River area also the Rainbow Snake is considered bisexual.[60]

Even more important are the polarities manifested in the Serpent's cosmic epiphanies and activities. Analyzing the belief of the Unambal and the Ungarinyin, we noticed that Ungud, the Primordial Snake, represents the mythical expression of the union of opposites.[61] Among many other tribes, the Rainbow Serpent is closely associated, on the one hand, with subterranean water and, on the other hand, with rain and, as such, with the sky. The great python of northern Australia "is the rainbow, which is his house or his trumpet, and is omniscient in the heaven and in the subterranean depths."[62] Apropos of the large rock paintings of the Rainbow Serpent, Elkin writes that they "express the desire for that *link with the world on top,* without which there would be no rain, and consequently no water present in the 'wells' and rock-holes."[63] As a cosmic figure, related to universal fertility, the Rainbow Serpent has both creative and destructive aspects: he brings the rains, but also

[59] W. E. H. Stanner, *On Aboriginal Religion* (Oceania Monograph No. 11 [Sydney, 1963], p. 87). Kunmanggu, the Rainbow Snake of the Murinbata, "may have been bi-sexual" (p. 96).

[60] Ronald M. Berndt (ed.), *Australian Aboriginal Art* (New York, 1964), p. 83.

[61] See Chapter 2, p. 79.

[62] Frederick D. McCarthy, *Australia's Aborigines: Their Life and Culture* (Melbourne, 1957), p. 119. The great mythical Water Serpent "is often the Rainbow-Serpent and like the latter, is in touch with the sky" (Elkin, *The Australian Aborigines,* p. 304).

[63] A. P. Elkin, "Art and Life," in R. M. Berndt (ed.), *Australian Aboriginal Art,* p. 19.

the catastrophic floods, and so on.[64] A. R. Radcliffe-Brown thought that the Rainbow Serpent could be considered "as occupying the position of the deity and perhaps the most important nature-deity."[65] But he is more than a "nature-deity." The Rainbow Serpent is related to women's mysteries, to sex and blood and after-death existence, and as we shall see, he also plays a central role in the initiations and mystical experiences of medicine men. In other words, he is an important deity because his structure has permitted the Rainbow Serpent to unite the opposites and finally to become a "totality." In different contexts, he could actualize a great number of religious possibilities which were latent in his all-embracing symbolism. We saw how the sexual symbolism of the Rainbow Serpent was overarticulated in the Kunapipi cult, and we shall see how other, and different, symbols gain primary roles in the medicine men's mystical experiences.

In sum, the quest for a naturistic genesis, or "origin," of a deity is meaningless. Any religious creation has, evidently, its source in life, ultimately in nature; but the identification of the source does not disclose to us the meaning of that particular creation. The Rainbow Snake is no more a rainbow than a snake. The "natural" meteorologic phenomenon and the "natural" reptilian species are religiously valuable

[64] See the bibliography on the Rainbow Serpent above, p. 79, n. 58. Vittorio Lanternari, *La Grande Festa* (Milan, 1959), pp. 329–49, considers the Australian Rainbow Serpent a "Lord of the Rain" and explains his myths and rituals as related exclusively to this cosmic phenomenon.

[65] A. R. Radcliffe-Brown, "The Rainbow-Serpent Myth in South-East Australia," *Oceania*, I (1930), 342–47, esp. 342. More recently, McCarthy (*Australia's Aborigines*, p. 129) expressed a similar opinion.

because they are related to a religious structure, that of the Rainbow Snake.

Initiation of Girls

As everywhere else in the world, the Australian girls' initiation is simpler than that of the boys.[66] At the first sign of puberty, the girl is separated from the main camp and sent for several days into seclusion. The break with the world of childhood is provoked by the physiological symptoms of menstruation. For this reason, the girl's initiation is largely individual. During the period of seclusion the girls are instructed by older women. They learn songs and specific myths, and especially the behavior and duties of married women. The concluding ceremony is simple but significant. Among some coastal tribes of northern Australia, the girl is painted with ochre and richly decorated by women. "At the climax, all the women escort her at dawn to a fresh water stream or lagoon."[67] After a ritual bath she is led in procession to the "main camp, amid a certain amount of acclamation, and is socially accepted as a woman."[68] The essential rite is a solemn exhibition of the girl to the community. She is *shown* to be an adult, that is, to be ready to assume the mode of being proper to women. It is a ceremonial proclamation that a mystery has been accomplished. "To show something ceremonially—a sign, an object, an animal—is to declare a sacred presence, to

[66] See Eliade, *Birth and Rebirth*, pp. 41 ff.; Bettelheim, *Symbolic Wounds*, pp. 239 ff.

[67] R. M. and C. H. Berndt, *The First Australians* (New York: Philosophical Library, 1954), p. 54.

[68] R. M. and C. H. Berndt, *Sexual Behavior in Western Arnhem Land*, pp. 89–91.

acclaim the miracle of a hierophany. This rite, which is so simple in itself, denotes a religious behaviour that is archaic. Very probably this ceremonial presentation of the initiated girl represents the earliest stage of the ceremony."[69]

In other places, the girl's initiation entails an artificial defloration followed by a ritual intercourse with a group of men.[70] H. Basedow mentions the "smoking ceremony" and ritual bathing among the Laragia and the Wogaidj.[71] In the Great Victoria Desert, after her seclusion the girl is taken into the bush and has her hymen cut. "Next day she is painted with red ochre and white clay and decorated with string necklets, and a pearlshell, with its 'life-giving' properties, restores her to life."[72]

Such operations as this artificial defloration and also the ceremonial group intercourse with the young girl are most probably mutilations and rituals invented by men and inflicted upon women at a certain stage of the men's growing authority. But, exactly as in the case of boys, the girl's puberty rites are only the beginning of her initiation. In some cases, one can even speak of gradual stages of initiation. Among the tribes of northwestern Australia, "with sexual maturity the girl may take part in the womens'

[69] Eliade, *Birth and Rebirth*, p. 43.

[70] Roth, *Ethnological Studies*, pp. 174 ff.; B. Spencer and F. J. Gillen, *The Native Tribes of Central Australia* (London: Macmillan, 1899), pp. 457 ff.; R. M. and C. H. Berndt, *The World of the First Australians*, p. 151.

[71] R. M. and C. H. Berndt, *The World of the First Australians*, p. 152.

[72] *Ibid.*, p. 152; Warner, *A Black Civilization*, p. 300, n. 15, writes that in northeastern Arnhem Land a girl, when she has had her first menses, is decorated with a flying fox (a large fruit bat) design associated with death.

secret corroborees. After she has a child, she may assist at the rites carried out for her female relatives. Later she gradually learns the songs that are *daragu* (= sacred) and *gunbu* (= taboo) to the men, and in old age she directs proceedings and becomes responsible for the handing on of her knowledge to the generation of women below her."[73] Childbirth especially constitutes a mystery. Phyllis Kaberry had more difficulty in collecting secret childbirth songs than she had in obtaining information from men in regard to the initiation of boys.[74] In most of the Northern Territory and neighboring regions, the women have their own secret rituals, to which men are not admitted.[75]

Women's Secret Ceremonies

Catherine Berndt was able to study two such women's ceremonies in the Victoria River district. The first one, *tjarada*, was "shown" to certain women, in dreams, by the two Mungamunga—fairylike creatures associated with the fertility cult of the Mother. They are said to be very attractive, although normally invisible, and to "possess supernatural powers, being able to go underground, and walk about the sky among the clouds: some women declare that they are associated with rain, and with the giant Rainbow Snake."[76] The woman remembers what she had seen in dream and re-enacts the ceremony, thus becoming its

[73] Phyllis M. Kaberry, *Aboriginal Woman, Sacred and Profane* (Philadelphia, 1939), p. 237.

[74] *Ibid.*, pp. 241 ff. On other women's secret ceremonies in rela-. tion to children, cf. Eliade, *Birth and Rebirth*, pp. 45 ff.

[75] Elkin, *The Australian Aborigines*, p. 193.

[76] Catherine H. Berndt, "Women's Changing Ceremonies in Northern Australia," *L'Homme: Cahiers d'ethnologie, de géographie et de linguistique*, I (Paris, 1950), 31.

lawful owner. To partake in the *tjarada* involves some danger; it implies contact with the sacred power of the Mother. The most important ritual object is a long pole, representing a snake ("Women's Changing Ceremonies," p. 33). The participants paint themselves in white and red ochre, with varied and beautiful patterns. The *tjarada* usually takes place on a special ground at some distance from the main camp. The men and young boys are warned not to approach the dancing place. Most of the songs are erotic in nature, but some of them refer to the Mother's journeys and adventures (pp. 40 ff.).

The second ceremony, *jawalju*, is considered to be "bigger" than *tjarada* because it is more closely associated with the dreaming period. More precautions are taken than in ordinary circumstances to prevent men from seeing what is going on. "*Jawalju* ceremonies are compared by the women to those which the men perform on the sacred ground; they all, it is said, have the same source and Dreaming background" (p. 45). Several dances re-enact the travels and activities of the Ancestral Being, or Beings, Ininguru, responsible for the ceremony. In the Dreaming period the Ininguru traveled across the "desert" country, but now they reside in the sky, although they still visit the earth to see what is going on (p. 44). Some of the songs are used for healing, others to stop a fight or a quarrel.[77] It is interest-

---

[77] Catherine Berndt also describes a recent "individual" ceremony, founded by a woman after a period of grave mental disturbances; her memory failed her, "like as if I been finished, dead" (*ibid.*, p. 53). During this "trance," Mungamunga appeared to her in dreams, showing her a "big" ceremony they were performing. She awoke one morning "clear-headed and apparently her usual self" (*ibid.*), and soon afterward she founded the cult. This "ecstatic" experience, implying a preliminary period of "madness,"

ing to note that the pattern of these women's secret ceremonies corresponds almost exactly to that of the ceremonies performed by men: the cult consists in the re-enactment of a series of rather banal incidents which took place in the mythical time.[78]

Though the women are not admitted to the male secret ceremonies, they do play a subsidiary role in some of them. For instance, they observe the prescribed taboos while the men are gathered for the secret rituals, they dance and chant in many preliminary stages, they answer ritual calls, and they are even present at some final episodes.[79] Of course, in the fertility cults of Arnhem Land the ceremonial role of women is more important. In the Maraian ceremony the women meet the men when they retire to the camp, and with their bodies painted they join them in dances around the ceremonial pole. In the Yabuduruwa cult of the Roper River district, the women are brought on the final night to within ten yards of the secret ritual ground. "No screen is raised between them and the lat-

unconsciousness, and visions, followed by a total psychomental recovery and a radical transformation of life (the passage from a "profane" to a "sacred" existence), is a characteristic syndrome of shamanistic experiences; cf. Eliade, *Shamanism*, esp. pp. 33 ff.

[78] When Catherine Berndt did her field work, the women's secret ceremonies were already rapidly decaying. Fewer and fewer women took part in the rituals ("Women's Changing Ceremonies," pp. 61 ff.). For many younger women the main interest of the chants and dances was exclusively erotic (cf., p. 59), and most of them used the ceremony as a magical means for their erotic life (p. 70). Incidentally, this transformation of a decaying religious cult into a magical operation is a process relevant for the under-standing of magic as a secondary phenomenon.

[79] Elkin, *The Australian Aborigines*, pp. 190–91; R. M. and C. H. Berndt, *The World of the First Australians*, pp. 214 ff.

ter."[80] They lie and sleep there knowing that a specific ritual object—related to the central figure of the myth—is buried superficially under them. They do not touch the sacred objects until they are awakened, but then they carry them ceremonially. "At this very time an important ritual is in progress and the women cannot but hear the rhythmic breathing as well as the gong beats. If they turned their heads as they jogged along they could see the actors. However, they light the iguana tails at the fire, and move off in a long sinuous line to the camp, conscious that they have played their part well."[81]

"It Belongs to Us Women"

There are also mythical traditions that indicate a more important role for the women in religious life in earlier times. Among some tribes, the (mythical) women are even considered the inventors of the rituals and the original owners of the sacred objects. Thus, among the Aranda, Spencer and Gillen found the souvenir of a time when women had more to do with sacred ceremonies than at present.[82] And Strehlow points out that in Aranda mythology the Ancestresses are "usually dignified and sometimes awe-inspiring figures, who enjoyed unlimited freedom of decision and action. Frequently they were much more powerful beings than their male associates, and the latter sometimes lived in constant terror of their mysterious su-

[80] Elkin, *The Australian Aborigines*, p. 191.

[81] *Ibid.*, p. 192. In Bathurst and Melville Islands, the women are still allowed to participate in sacred rites; cf. Charles P. Mountford, *The Tiwi* (London, 1958); De Leeuwe, *op. cit.*, XIV, 339.

[82] Spencer and Gillen, *The Northern Tribes of Central Australia*, pp. 195, 196.

pernatural strength. These feminine ancestors used to carry about *tjurungas*, and they instituted sacred ceremonies. Today many chants are still sung in their honor by groups of men. . . . These men regard themselves as the natural 'trustees' of all the sacred *tjurungas* pertaining to the women of their group."[83]

Moreover, there are some allusions to the role played earlier by women in the rites of circumcision. For example, an Aranda myth relates that the women once found the boys ready for circumcision; they seized them, put them on their shoulders, and performed the operation.[84] Another tradition points out that in the beginning the men made use of fire sticks to circumcise the boys, with fatal consequences, until the women threw a sharp piece of flint up to them.[85] Among some tribes, the foreskin of the initiated boy is given to his sister, who then dries it, anoints it with ochre, and suspends it from her neck.[86]

---

[83] Strehlow, *Aranda Traditions*, p. 94. But now the men look down upon their own women. "Our women are of no use at our ceremonial gatherings. They are altogether ignorant of the sacred *tjurungas*. They have fallen from the estate of our great feminine ancestors. Why, we do not know" (*ibid.*).

[84] Spencer and Gillen, *The Native Tribes of Central Australia*, p. 442.

[85] R. M. and C. H. Berndt, "A Preliminary Report on Field Work in the Ooldea Region, Western South Australia," *Oceania*, Vols. XII–XV (1942–45); see XIII (1943), 257. But see also n. 47, above. Bettelheim (*Symbolic Wounds*, p. 170) has quoted similar myths of circumcision as a feminine invention from New Hebrides. The same tradition is found among the Bambuti: circumcision was discovered by a woman, who supposedly saw the apes practicing it (P. Schebesta, *Les Pygmées du Congo Belge* [Brussels, 1951], p. 266).

[86] Spencer and Gillen, *The Native Tribes of Central Australia*, p. 251; cf. also Spencer and Gillen, *The Northern Tribes of Cen-*

Even more intriguing are the traditions that at the beginning the ritual objects were discovered and owned by
women. In a Wiknatara myth, the first bull-roarer was
twirled by two young girls, who said: "It belongs to us
women, really we have found it! But no matter! We leave
it for the men. It is they who will always use it!"[87] In the
Western Desert south of Balgo, the mythical women possessed all the sacred rituals before they were taken from
them by the men. Likewise, in western Arnhem Land the
ubar ceremony belonged in the beginning only to women.[88]
The Djanggawul myth in northeastern Arnhem Land tells
how the two Sisters built a shelter and hung their baskets
in it full of sacred emblems. While they were away, their
Brother and his companion stole the baskets and began
performing the ritual. The women "were too frightened
to go near that place, fearful not of the men but of the
power of the sacred songs. The men had taken from them
not only these songs, and the emblems, but also the power
to perform sacred ritual, a power which had formerly belonged only to the Sisters. Before that, men had nothing.
The myth continues: The elder Sister said, '. . . Men can
do it now, they can look after it . . . We know every-

---

tral Australia, pp. 352, 368, etc., for other examples of the relation
between women and circumcision (or subincision). Cf. Bettleheim,
Symbolic Wounds, pp. 159 ff.

[87] U. H. McConnel, "Myths of the Wikmunkan and Wiknatara
Tribes," *Oceania*, VI (1936), 68. In a Wikmunkan myth the
women say: "this is a bull-roarer, we found it! We women! It is
we who have found it!" (p. 82).

[88] R. M. and C. H. Berndt, *The World of the First Australians*,
p. 215. "Then we had nothing: no sacred objects, no sacred ceremonies, the women had everything" (R. M. Berndt, *Kunapipi*, p. 8;
cf. also pp. 55, 59).

thing. We have really lost nothing, because we remember it all, and we can let them have that small part. Aren't we still sacred, even if we have lost the baskets?' "[89]

Another myth tells how at the beginning the Ganabuda women had all the sacred things, while men had nothing. "But one man, Djalaburu, creeping close and watching them secretly one night, discovered that they kept their power (*maia*) under their armbands. He succeeded in stealing this. Next morning the women tried to swing their bull-roarers, but they could hardly manage to do so: they had lost their power. After that, Djalaburu led them down to where the men were; the men went up to where the women had been, and took over their responsibility for attending to sacred matters."[90]

What is significant in these traditions is the fact that the (mythical) women accepted the consequences of the theft, that is to say, the passing of the magico-religious powers from their hands into the men's. In some cases, the saving

[89] R. M. and C. H. Berndt, *The World of the First Australians*, p. 216. Cf. *ibid.*, p. 239, the ritual re-enactment of the theft. The complete text of the myth is in R. M. Berndt, *Djanggawul* (London, 1952), pp. 38–41. Another version is in Chaseling, *op. cit.*, pp. 133–34: "In those days women were the guardians of ceremonial secrets, and their male children led a vague, indolent existence. But when the ancestresses began preparing for the first great intertribal ceremonies, their sons became jealous." They stole the "totems," and when the Djanggawul Sisters tried to recover them, they were driven away by the power of the men's ritual singing and dancing. The Sisters said: "No matter, let the men keep the totems," and so it has been ever since. See also Charles P. Mountford (ed.), *Records of the American-Australian Scientific Expedition to Arnhem Land*, I (Melbourne, 1956), 269 ff.

[90] R. M. and C. H. Berndt, *The World of the First Australians*, p. 224.

mystical knowledge is purposely communicated by the Ancestress in dreams. Such was the mode of transmission from the Wauwalak Sisters to the Wongar ancestors: they taught them all the secret dances and chants while they were in a deep sleep. They told them: "We are giving you this dream so you can remember these important things."[91]

Similar myths relating how the women possessed the ritual objects and cultic scenarios are to be found elsewhere, especially in Melanesia and South America.[92] As was to be expected, depth psychologists accorded considerable attention to such mythological traditions. Some authors even thought that these myths mirror a primordial situation that was once universal. The historian of religions is confronted with a different problem. The first thing to be considered is the nature of the sacred objects and rituals said to have been originally owned by women: they are "totemic" emblems (type *ranga*), bull-roarers, masks (in South America), ceremonial songs and dances related to sexuality and fertility, or a ritual operation (circumcision) claimed to have been discovered, perfected, or suggested to men by women. All these sacred objects and secret rituals have something in common: they are *powerful*, somehow "magical" instruments, for they can incorporate or represent supernatural forces (e.g., bull-roarers), or, more precisely, they can *compel* the incarnation of such supernatural forces (e.g., the masks). They are all related to the epiphanies of life (blood, sex, fertility) or to the "powers" deriving from

[91] Warner, *A Black Civilization*, p. 249.
[92] See Eliade, *Birth and Rebirth*, pp. 29 ff. and p. 145, n. 50; F. Speiser, "Die Frau als Erfinderin von Kultgeräten in Melanesien," *Schweizerische Zeitschrift für Psychologie und ihre Anwendungen*, III (1944), 46–64.

them. However, *no important religious doctrines—and no significant cosmological myths—are said to have been discovered by, or to have been the original property of, women.* In sum, these traditions tell us that at some time in the past men stole, or received, from women a number of powerful symbols and that this incident marked a radical change in both sexes: from a subordinate position, men became the masters.

But, judging from the Australian myths, this radical transformation has been candidly accepted by women. We must also keep in mind that the theme of the theft is restricted to the fertility cults of Arnhem Land. In other words, these myths tell us that men began to perform the women's secret ceremonies after stealing—or receiving—the sacred objects or the ritual scenarios. But, as we have already noticed, the Arnhem Land fertility cults are the result of rather recent influences from Melanesia. That is to say, the mythical motif "it belongs to us women" reflects "historical" changes and not a "primordial" situation. Similarly, no conclusion can be deduced from the myths that proclaim the role of women in the discovery or the perfection of circumcision, and this for the simple reason that, in Australia, this operation is "a comparatively recent custom which has spread from the northwest,"[93] that is, the same Melanesian zone of influence from which the fertility cults were diffused. Consequently, no general theory of the "origin" and the original meaning and function of circumcision can be based on the Australian evidence.

Nevertheless, some of these myths indicate a process that really took place and considerably modified the Australian

[93] Elkin, *The Australian Aborigines*, p. 138. Also among the Bambuti (cf. n. 85, above), the circumcision is recent.

religions. The Aranda traditions, for example, express quite clearly the recognition of a more powerful sacrality of women in mythical times. This means that earlier there was a stronger religious collaboration between the two sexes. It is probable that the excessive secrecy of most male religious ceremonies does not correspond to an original situation but represents a later development. We have already noticed the tendency of the Australian initiation scenario to become a *Männerbund*-type of secret society. In this case, the related myths convey the women's loss of their previous religious "powers." In regard to "it belongs to us women" mythology, it certainly represents a characteristic episode of northern Australia's sacred history, but its basic elements are to be found beyond that area. They reflect the dramatic impact made by the inclusion of sexual and fertility rites into an earlier religious system. Almost all the ritual scenarios dependent on this myth emphasize a rather ambivalent attitude to women and women's mysteries. This may be explained as a consequence of the drastic innovations brought about by the Melanesian influences. But, on the other hand, one must not forget that long before all these more or less recent innovations there always existed a tension between the two types of sacrality, masculine and feminine, a reciprocal envy and jealousy of the other sex's mysteries, which explains why so many feminine magical symbols and prestiges were appropriated by shamans and medicine men, and vice versa.[94]

[94] See, *inter alia*, Eliade, *Birth and Rebirth*, pp. 78 ff.

CHAPTER 4

The Medicine Men and
Their Supernatural Models

"Men of High Degree"

Provided he pursues his religious instruction, every male hopes to learn, in his old age, the sacred history of the tribe. This ultimately means re-establishing contact with the actors of a sacred history and, consequently, partaking of their creative powers. But, as everywhere else in the world, so is it in Australia that man's relations with the sphere of the sacred are not uniform. There are always some exceptionally gifted individuals longing, or destined, to become "religious specialists." These medicine men, doctors, shamans, or, as Elkin aptly calls them, "men of high degree," play a central role in the life of the tribe.[1] They cure the

[1] The most important monograph on Australian medicine men is Elkin's *Aboriginal Men of High Degree.* Helmut Petri's "Der australische Medizinmann," Part I, *Annali Lateranensi* (Città del Vaticano), XVI (1952), 159–317; Part II, XVII (1953), 157–225, is an original and well-documented study (though apparently the author did not know Elkin's book). Marcel Mauss's "L'Origine des pouvoirs magiques dans les sociétés australiennes" (Paris: Ecole Patrique des Hautes Etudes, 1904), 1–55 (reprinted in Henri Hubert and Marcel Mauss, *Mélanges d'histoire des religions* [2d ed.; Paris, 1929], pp. 131–87), is still valuable for the critical discussion of the older documents. Curiously enough, in the section dedicated to Australian religions (*Der Ursprung der Gottesidee,* III [Münster, 1931], 565–1114), Wilhelm Schmidt devoted only a few pages to the medicine men of the southeastern tribes (Kurnai, pp.

sick, defend the community against black magic, discover those responsible for premature deaths, and perform important functions in the initiation ceremonies.

But the most specific characteristic of the medicine man is his relation with the Supernatural Beings and the other heroes of the tribe's sacred history. He is the only one who is *really* able to recover the glorious conditions of the mythical Ancestors, the only one who can do what the Ancestors did, for instance, fly through the air, ascend to heaven, travel underground, disappear and reappear. Moreover, only the medicine man can encounter the Supernatural Beings and converse with them, and only he can see the spirits and the ghosts of the dead. In sum, only the medicine man succeeds in surpassing his human condition, and consequently he is able to behave like the spiritual beings, or, in other words, to partake of the modality of a Spiritual Being.

As in so many other parts of the world, the medicine man in Australia is not the product of a spontaneous creation; he is "made," either by Supernatural Beings or by the medicine men of his tribe. One becomes a medicine man by inheriting the profession, by "call" or election, or by personal quest. But whatever way he has taken, a postulant is not recognized as a medicine man until he has been accepted by a certain number of "men of high degree" and

---

635–38; Kulin, pp. 709–12; Wiradjuri-Kamilaroi, pp. 902–5). The rest of the literature will be quoted in passing as we proceed in our study. Some of the material published by Ronald M. Berndt, "Wuradjeri Magic and 'Clever Men,'" Part I, *Oceania*, XVII (1946–47), 327–65; Part II, *ibid.*, XVIII (1947–48), 60–86, was already used or summarized by Elkin in his *Aboriginal Men of High Degree*, from Berndt's field notes. We shall therefore refer to both sources.

been taught by some of them, and, above all, until he has undergone a more or less spectacular initiation. In most cases the initiation consists of an ecstatic experience, during which the candidate meets Supernatural Beings, undergoes certain operations, and undertakes ascents to heaven and descents to the subterranean world.

All these ecstatic experiences, as well as the scenarios of the "quest," follow traditional patterns. For instance, the aspirant to the profession goes to sleep in isolated places, especially near the grave of a medicine man, and he is expected to have visions or even initiatory revelations similar to those of all the "elected." The basic experience is an inspired vision, during which the future medicine man encounters the Supernatural Being who will bestow upon him the sacred powers. The meeting is always dramatic, even in cases where (as among the southeastern tribes) the "making" does not include a ritual "killing" of the postulant (although still, even in such cases, the transmutation of the postulant's mode of being—from a human state to a "spiritual" one—implies, as we shall presently see, a "death" followed by a resurrection). The Supernatural Beings, or their representatives, radically change the bodily condition of the aspirant (by inserting sacred substances, etc.), and at the same time teach him how to bear himself as a "spirit" (how to fly, etc.). Among the tribes where the "making" comprises a ritual killing, the Supernatural Beings or their representatives perform certain operations on the lifeless body of the candidate; they remove the insides and substitute new ones, inserting also sacred substances, quartz or pearl-shells. Whatever the nature of the ecstatic experience, the aspirant comes back to life as another person: he has seen the Supernatural Beings face to face and been "made" and taught by them. What remains to be learned from the old masters is now of a more or less technical nature. His mystical initiation introduced him to a spiritual universe which henceforth will be his *real* world.

Initiation of a Wiradjuri Medicine Man

Ultimately, the three ways of becoming a medicine man —(1) inheriting the profession, (2) "call" or election, (3) personal "quest"—result in a specific experience, without which a change in the novice's mode of being would not take place. This can be clearly seen in the process of initiation. Where the profession is inherited, the father carefully prepares his son before provoking the rapture which will transform his life. Howitt reports a characteristic example of a Wiradjuri medicine man who had been initiated by his father. When he was still a young boy, his father took him into the bush and placed two large quartz crystals against his breast. They vanished into his body, and he felt them going through him "like warmth." The old man also gave him "some things like quartz crystals in water. They looked like ice and the water tasted sweet." After that, the boy could see ghosts. When he was about ten years old, after having his tooth out in the age-grading ceremony, his father showed him a piece of quartz crystal in his hand, "and when I looked at it he [his father] went down into the ground and I saw him come up all covered with red dust. It made me very frightened." The father asked him to try to produce a piece of crystal, and the boy brought one up (probably from his own body).

Then the father led his son through a hole in the ground to a grave. Going inside, the boy saw a dead man who rubbed him all over to make him "clever"; the dead man also gave him some crystals. When the father and son came out, the father pointed to a tiger snake and told the boy that it was his secret totem (*budjan*) and that from then on it would also be his son's. "There was a string tied to the tail of the snake, and extending to us." It was one of the strings which the medicine men draw out of themselves, of which more will be said later. The father took hold of the string, saying, "Let us follow him." The snake went through several tree trunks, and finally to a tree with a great swelling around its roots. There the snake went down into the ground, and they followed it coming up inside the tree, which was hollow.

After they came out from the tree, the snake took them into a great hole in the ground. Here there were many snakes which rubbed themselves against the boy to make him a "clever man." The father then said:

We will go up to Baiame's camp. He got astride of a Mauir (thread) and put me on another, and we held by each other's arms. At the end of the thread was Wombu, the bird of Baiame. We went through the clouds, and on the other side was the sky. We went through the place where the Doctors go through, and it kept opening and shutting very quickly. My father said that, if it touched a Doctor when he was going through, it would hurt his spirit, and when he returned home he would sicken and die. On the other side we saw Baiame sitting in his camp. He was a very great old man with a long beard. He sat with his legs under him and from his shoulders extended two great quartz crystals to the sky above him. There were also numbers of the boys of Baiame and of his people, who are birds and beasts.[2]

[2] Howitt, *The Native Tribes of South-East Australia*, pp. 406–8. See also the visit to heaven of a Wuradjeri (= Wiradjuri) medi-

In sum, the physical transformation of the novice begins with his assimilation of quartz crystals. After taking some of these crystals into his body, the boy can see the "spirits," invisible to noninitiates, and can travel underground. The dead man in the grave, who probably was a former medicine man, likewise gave him quartz crystals, and also rubbed against his body, as the snakes did later in order to infuse him with their powers. The initiation was completed by an ascension to heaven, where the boy and his father saw Baiame with two great quartz crystals extending from his shoulders. We shall repeatedly encounter these motifs, and their meanings will become clearer as we proceed with the description of different types of initiation. For the moment, let us add that, according to the beliefs of the Euahlayi, Baiame is fixed in the crystal rock on which he sits. The medicine men reach his celestial abode after a laborious journey: they climb a mountain for four days, and when they reach the top they drink from a spring and are reinvigorated. There they are greeted by Baiame's spirit messengers, who finally present the requests of the medicine men to the enthroned High Being.[3] The celestial structure of Baiame is repeatedly emphasized; he is even imagined as fastened in the crystal-like vault of heaven.

---

cine man through a small aperture revealed at intervals in the revolving two walls of a cleft, described by Berndt, "Wuradjeri Magic," Part I, p. 362. The 'hole in the sky' is known also among the Kurnai; cf. Howitt, *op. cit.*, p. 389. This is the widely known initiatory motif of Symplegades; cf. Eliade, *Birth and Rebirth*, pp. 64–66, 130.

[3] K. L. Parker, *The Euahlayi Tribe* (London, 1905), pp. 25 ff., 35–36; *idem, More Legendary Tales* (London, 1898), pp. 84 ff. Cf. Elkin, *Aboriginal Men of High Degree*, pp. 102 ff.

Baiame and the Medicine Men

The role of Baiame in the making of the Wiradjuri medicine men, which can be only inferred from Howitt's description, seems to be, on the contrary, decisive according to the data collected by Ronald Berndt at Menindee, in New South Wales. Already at an early age the postulant was trained by a "doctor," preferably his father or grandfather. The doctor's spirit took the boy's spirit with him at night, up to the sky, while the medicine man climbed skyward on a magical cord to make rain. When the boy was twelve years old, the doctor "sang" into him his assistant totem. Thus, by the time of his tribal initiation the boy knew already some of the fundamental principles of his future profession, "but he did not possess the power, insight or control to work magic." He obtained all these through a ritual and a spiritual experience. When he was between twenty and thirty years of age, Baiame informed the postulant's teacher in a dream that he would initiate the young man. "Similar dreams occurred to other guardians in the same or adjacent tribes. . . . They all met at a fixed time with their candidates at a sacred place. The latter were seated on a long 'couch' of leaves, while the doctors sang to summon Baiame. He came from out of the air towards the seated groups. He looked like any doctor, except for the light which radiated from his eyes. Coming up to each postulant, he said: 'I'll make you,' and caused sacred powerful water, said to be liquified quartz, to fall on him."

This water spread all over the postulants and was completely absorbed by them. Then feathers emerged from the candidates' arms, which in two days grew into wings. In the meantime Baiame had disappeared, and the postulants were instructed by their masters in the significance of the sacred water and the feathers. The symbolism of celestial ascension is evident in the case of both of these mystical objects. Indeed, the next stage consists in each postulant going personally to meet Baiame. The Supernatural Being teaches him to fly and also how to use quartz crystals. "Baiame sang a piece [of quartz] into his forehead so that he would be able to see right into things. He also took from his own body a flame, which he sang into the postulant's chest, and taught the latter how he could release it. Then, directed back to his camp, he flew, sang off his wings, walked in and sat alongside of his guardian, with whom he discussed his experience."

The third experience takes place after the "making." All the new doctors go to a sacred site and there lie on a couch of leaves. "After the 'singing,' Baiame appeared, placed a cord in 'U' fashion across the chest and down the legs of each of them, and sang it into them. Henceforward, this was to be used as a spider uses his web. Baiame then bid them farewell and went away." The newly made doctors then remain in seclusion for two or three days, practicing magical displays.

According to another account given to Berndt, the ecstatic experience of the "call" can take place without any prearranging or conditioning. One would-be medicine man was hunting when "he found himself dragged down and across to a strange country on the other side of the sea. Then Baiame carried him off to a very large cave, where he pierced him with his 'X-ray' eyes and, looking into his mind, asked whether he had been made a man, and also prepared by his father to receive Baiame's power and knowledge." The answer being affirmative, Baiame made him a doctor in the way already described.[4]

Thus it seems that, whereas the doctors only prepare the young man for his future profession, the actual initiation is effectuated by Baiame. We know too little about the actual making of the medicine man[5] to be able to distinguish between the purely visionary and the concrete ritual elements of the above scenario. It is probable that at a certain moment the postulant, in a more or less hallucinatory state, takes part in a ritual in which Baiame is impersonated by one of the old doctors. But what is relevant for the understanding of the southeast Australian medicine man is the fact that the source of the mystical power is related to a celestial High Being and that the initiation consists in the appropriation of his various prestiges, the first and foremost of which is the ability to fly. According to the Wiradjuri tradition, when Baiame left the earth, he assembled all the doctors and told them that he "made" them in order to carry on his work once he returned to his home.[6]

---

[4] Elkin, *Aboriginal Men*, pp. 96–98. A more detailed description of this initiation was published by Berndt, "Wuradjeri Magic," Part I, pp. 334–38.

[5] We must always keep in mind an admonition coming from such an experienced fieldworker as Elkin: "It is difficult to obtain complete knowledge of the initiation of adult males into full membership of their secret life. Judging from fresh bits of information that I acquire from time to time, *I doubt whether we have, in any one instance, been admitted into all the secrets of the ritual and knowledge.* But if this is difficult, it is more so when we come to inquire into that ritual through which a medicine man acquired power. Those who are not members of the profession know little about it" (Elkin, *The Australian Aborigines*, p. 300; my italics).

[6] Berndt, "Wuradjeri Magic," Part I, pp. 334 ff.

An Initiation Scenario

The essential elements of the southeast initiation scenario seem to be (1) the bright cave, (2) the miraculous feathers, (3) the flight, (4) the quartz crystals, (5) the magic rope. All of them are connected with the sky and the celestial powers.

The celestial element seems least evident in the symbolism of the cave. We shall, in fact, quote later on some examples from central Australia in which the cave is charged with an opposite symbolism. But among the southeastern tribes its celestial character is clearly emphasized by the luminosity of the initiation cave. To add only one other example, a Kurnai medicine man (*mulla-mullung*) told Howitt that, in a dream, his dead father and many other old men carried him through the air over the sea, and set him at the front of a big rock like the front of a house.

I noticed that there was something like an opening in the rock. My father tied something over my eyes and led me inside. I knew this because I heard the rocks make a sound as of knocking behind me. Then he uncovered my eyes, and I found that I was in a place as bright as day, and all the old men were round about. My father showed me a lot of shining, bright things, like glass, on the walls, and told me to take some. I took one and held it tight in my hand. When we went out again my father taught me how to make these things go into my legs, and how I could pull them out again.[7]

The cave is bright because it is covered with quartz crystals, that is, it ultimately partakes of the mystical nature of the sky.

[7] Howitt, *The Native Tribes of South-East Australia*, pp. 408 ff.

As for the wings and feathers, their ascensional symbolism is evident. The growing of wings as a result of a mystical initiation is a well-known motif, found also in the high religions. Thus, for instance, the Taoists believe that when a man obtains the *tao*, feathers begin to grow on his body.[8] For Plato also, a man "beholds the beauty of this world, is reminded of true beauty, and his wings begin to grow" (*Phaedrus* 249*e*), for "aforetimes the whole soul was furnished with wings" (251*b*). This imagery was repeatedly utilized and elaborated by the Neo-Platonists, the Christian fathers, and the Gnostics.[9] Of course, these images are related to the conception of the soul as a volatile spiritual substance, comparable to and identified with birds and butterflies. But it is significant to find already in an archaic religion a similar scenario of mystical initiation conceived as an ascension, that is, acquisition of the capacity to "fly" like a bird. Flight is one of the most widespread, and probably the most archaic, expressions of transcending the human condition and "becoming a spirit."[10]

The journey to heaven is characteristic to the making of the medicine man among most tribes of southeast Australia. The Wurunjeri postulant is carried by the spirits through

[8] Max Kaltenmark, *Le Lie-sien tchouan: Biographies légendaires des immortels taoïstes de l'antiquité* (Peking, 1953), p. 20. See also Eliade, *Shamanism*, pp. 403, 450 ff.

[9] Cf., *inter alia*, P. Boyancé, "La Religion astrale de Platon à Cicéron," *Revue des Etudes grecques*, LXV (1952), 321–30; A. Orbe, "Variaciones gnosticas sobre las Alas del Alma," *Gregorianum*, XXXV (1954), 24–35; J. Daniélou, *Message évangélique et culture hellénistique* (Paris, 1961), pp. 116 ff.

[10] Cf. M. Eliade, *Mythes, rêves et mystères* (Paris, 1957), pp. 132 ff. (= *Myths, Dreams and Mysteries* [New York, 1960], pp. 99 ff.).

a hole in the sky to Bunjil, from whom he receives his powers.[11] The Kurnai distinguish between the medicine men (*mulla-mullung*) and the *birra-ark*, who "combined the functions of the seer, the spirit-medium, and the bard" (Howitt, p. 389). The medicine man is initiated by *mrarts*, or spirits in the bush, and has to wear a nose bone which the spirits grasp to convey him to the clouds. It is said that, preceded by the spirits, the medicine man climbs through a hole in the sky land; there he sees people dancing and singing, and on returning he teaches the Kurnai these songs and dances.[12] The *kunki* of the Dieiri can fly up to the sky by means of a hair cord; they have direct communication both with the Supernatural Beings and the mythical Ancestors (*mura-muras*).[13] According to Berndt, the medicine men south of Murray could travel through the air on a cord projected from their own bodies; they also could take any form and make themselves invisible.[14] Among several tribes of southwestern Victoria, the ascension of the medicine man to heaven seems to have been the central element in the cure of a patient.[15]

[11] Howitt, *The Native Tribes of South-East Australia*, p. 405; see also pp. 389 ff.

[12] *Ibid.,* p. 389. On the *birra-ark*, the *mulla-mullung*, and the *bunjil* of the Kurnai, see now Engelbert Stiglmayr, "Schamanismus in Australia," *Wiener Völkerkundliche Mitteilungen*, V (1957), 161–90. Also the Wongaibon medicine man could visit the sky land; Cf. A. L. P. Cameron, "Notes on Some Tribes of New South Wales," *Journal of the Royal Anthropological Institute*, XIV (1885), 360–61.

[13] Howitt, *The Native Tribes of South-East Australia*, pp. 358–59. Cf. also Elkin, *Aboriginal Men of High Degree*, p. 119.

[14] Elkin, *Aboriginal Men of High Degree*, p. 85; Berndt, "Wuradjeri Magic," Part I, pp. 356 ff.; Part II, p. 79.

[15] Elkin, *Aboriginal Men of High Degree*, p. 85.

But the medicine man's ability to fly is known also in other parts of the continent. Among the Aranda, for instance, the doctors assume the form of eagle-hawks, which Elkin correctly interprets in terms of their power to travel through the air.[16] In Kimberley, the doctors visit the dead by going up to the sky on a string.[17] And the close relationship between the medicine man and the Rainbow Serpent also implies the former's ascension to heaven. For the moment we may quote an initiation from the Forest River District, northern Kimberley, where the motif of ascension is integrated in a scenario different from the one presented above. The medicine men's power ultimately comes from Ungud, the Rainbow Serpent, but it is a "fully qualified practitioner" who performs the initiation. The master carries the postulant to the sky either by using a string which "hangs down from the sky, with cross pieces on which the two men sit," or by taking the form of a skeleton, sitting and pulling himself up with an arm-over-arm motion on a rope. In this second case, the postulant had been previously transformed into an infant; the medicine man put him in a pouch and fastened it to his body. When near the vault "the latter throws the postulant out of the pouch on to the sky, thus making him 'dead.' Having reached the sky, the 'doctor' inserts into the young man some little rainbow snakes and some quartz crystals." After bringing him back to earth, the doctor introduces more of these magical substances into the postulant through the navel, and finally awakens him with a magic stone. "The

---

[16] B. Spencer and F. J. Gillen, *Native Tribes of Central Australia* (London, 1899), pp. 522 ff.; Elkin, *Aboriginal Men of High Degree*, p. 121.

[17] Elkin, *Aboriginal Men of High Degree*, p. 138.

young man returns to his normal size, if he had been changed, and the next day he tries himself to go to the sky." His instruction proper begins after this ecstatic experience.[18] Elkin rightly remarks that the reduction to infant size and the resemblance between the doctor's pouch and the kangaroo's indicate that this is a ritual of rebirth.[19]

Initiation by Being Swallowed by a Monster

An initiation reported by Berndt from the Western Desert tribes of South Australia presents a similar scenario, but considerably developed. Mourned as dead because he is going to be "cut into pieces," the postulant goes to a certain water hole. There two medicine men blindfold him and throw him into the jaws of the great Snake, Wonambi, who swallows him. The postulant remains in the Serpent's belly for an indefinite time. Finally the two medicine men give the Serpent two kangaroo rats, whereupon he ejects the postulant, throwing him high into the air. He falls "alongside a certain rock-hole," and the doctors set out in search of him, "visiting and camping at each of a series of rock-holes until they find him at the last one." But he has been reduced to the size of an infant, "Wonambi having made him like that." (The initiatory theme of regression to the embryonic condition in the monster's belly, homologous with the maternal womb, is apparent here.) The doctors take the baby in their arms and fly back to their camp.

After this consecration, which is pre-eminently mystical because it is performed by a Supernatural Being, the initiation proper begins, in which a number of old masters play the principal role. Placed within a circle of fires, the baby

[18] *Ibid.*, pp. 139–40.
[19] *Ibid.*, p. 140. Cf. Eliade, *Birth and Rebirth*, p. 160, n. 72.

postulant rapidly grows and recovers his adult size. He declares that he knows the Serpent well, that they are even friends, for he stayed in his belly for some time. Then comes a period of seclusion, during which the postulant meditates and converses with spirits. One day the doctors take him to the bush and smear his body with red ochre. "He is made to lie full-length on his back before fires, and is said to be a dead man. The head doctor proceeds to break his neck and his wrists, and to dislocate the joints at the elbows, the upper thighs, the knees and ankles. . . . Actually, the operator does not amputate each part properly, but rather makes a mark with the stone." The doctor puts into each cut a life-giving shell; he also stuffs shells into his ears, so that the postulant will be able to understand and speak to spirits, strangers, and animals, and "into his forehead, so that it may be turned in all directions." His stomach too is stuffed with shells, "in order that he may have renewed life, and become invulnerable to attack by any weapons." Then he is "sung" by the medicine men, and revives. All return to the main camp, where the new doctor is tested: the fully initiated men throw their spears at him; but because of the shells with which he is stuffed, he is not harmed.[20]

This example is representative of a highly elaborate initi-

---

[20] Elkin, *Aboriginal Men of High Degree*, pp. 112 ff.; R. and C. Berndt, "A Preliminary Report of Field-Work in the Ooldea Region, Western South Australia," *Oceania*, XIV (1943), 56–61; cf. Eliade, *Birth and Rebirth*, pp. 97–98. Other examples of postulants being swallowed by a snake are in C. Strehlow, *Die Aranda und Loritjastämme in Zentral-Australien* (Frankfurt, a. M., 1908), II, 9–10; Géza Roheim, *The Eternal Ones of the Dream* (New York, 1945), pp. 184 ff.; Elkin, *Aboriginal Men of High Degree*, p. 112 (the Wirangu tribe).

ation. We can recognize two principal initiatory themes in it: (1) being swallowed by a monster and (2) bodily dismemberment—of which only the second is peculiar to the making of medicine men. But, although he undergoes a return to the womb, the postulant does not die in the Serpent's belly, for he is able to remember his sojourn there. The real initiatory death is brought about by the old doctors, and in the manner reserved for medicine men: dismemberment of the body, change of organs, introduction of magical substances.

"Passing Through the Waters"

In some cases an initiation through fire is completed by a second ordeal, "passing through the water." Elkin studied such a "making" of the medicine man among the Kattang-speaking peoples who occupied the northern shore of Port Stephens. The ceremony continues for six months. When a candidate has "died," he is thrown on the fire by the old masters and kept there until he is completely consumed. One such candidate declared later on that he "felt" nothing, because, comments Elkin, "he was in a condition approaching hypnosis, though he could see what was there." Eventually, "he was restored by the old men putting their hands on his shoulder, after which he was shown secret symbols and taught their meaning. As a result the man became a new personality and, as it were, no longer belonged to the earth but to the sky-world." According to Elkin, it does not seem that all candidates went through this ceremony, which in any case was not sufficient to make a "clever man." To reach that stage, the neophyte had "to pass through the water." He is thrown into a sacred water hole, from which he looks up to Gulambré, the Sky Being, and asks for power. Eventually the medicine men bring him out and put their hands on his shoulder to restore him to consciousness. The initiation continues in the bush; the candidate swallows quartz crystals, which he will later project when performing magical tricks. As a result, the newly made "clever man" is able to go up to the sky in dream and also to cure sick people.[21]

Among the Laitu-Laitu tribe the medicine man is able to go to the bottom of a lake or a river and stay there for days near the spirit Konikatine. He returns "with his eyes bloodshot, and his cloak covered with ooze," and reports his experiences. Elkin rightly infers that the descent "was most likely part of the initiation, as well as henceforth a privilege and necessity, and represents the period of seclusion in which powers were given."[22] The lakes and water holes are also the domain of spirits and ghosts. The descent to the bottom of the lake signifies a *descensus ad inferos*. As a matter of fact, the Laitu-Laitu medicine man is "made" by sleeping for a month on a hut over the grave of a doctor.[23]

The Ritual "Killing" of the Postulant

In many of the initiations described above, the future medicine man undergoes a symbolic death followed by

[21] Elkin, *Aboriginal Men of High Degree*, p. 91.
[22] *Ibid.*, p. 93. W. E. Roth reported that Brisbane medicine men dove to the bottom of deep pools to obtain magical quartz ("Superstitions, Magic and Medicine," *North Queensland Ethnography*, No. 5 [1903], p. 30). Of course, all these symbols and rituals are related to the Rainbow Snake.
[23] Elkin, *Aboriginal Men of High Degree*, p. 93. Also the Clarence River doctors sleep on graves (p. 91). Cf. other examples, (pp. 105–6).

resurrection. As we have seen (cf. above, Chapter III), this is the initiatory pattern par excellence. In central Australia and other parts of the continent, the initiatory death is expressed in terms of the "killing" of the postulant and the insertion of magical substances into his body. This scenario is abundantly attested by the sources.[24] We shall limit our survey to a few characteristic examples. Among the tribes of the Warburton Ranges (western Australia), initiation

[24] Already in 1798, Colonel Collins reported that among the Port Jackson tribes one becomes a medicine man by sleeping on a grave. "The spirit of the deceased would visit him, seize him by the throat, and opening him, take out his bowels, which he replaced, and the wound closed up" (cited by Howitt, *The Native Tribes of South-East Australia*, p. 405). Among the Wotjobaluk and Jupagalk, a Supernatural Being named Ngetya, who lives in the bush, cuts open the postulant's side and inserts quartz crystals (*ibid.*, p. 104; Elkin, *Aboriginal Men of High Degree*, p. 85). To make a medicine man, the Euahlayi carry the neophyte to a cemetery and leave him there, bound for several nights. Eventually a man comes with a stick; he thrusts the stick into the young man's head and puts a magical stone the size of a lemon into the wound. Then the spirits appear and intone magical and initiatory songs to teach him the art of healing (Parker, *The Euahlayi Tribe*, pp. 25–26). Among the Maitakundi tribe, the initiatory murder is effectuated by the master himself: he "kills" the postulant, throws him in a water hole, and leaves him there for four days. Then he takes him out, puts him between fires, and smokes the body quite dry (Roth, quoted by Elkin, *Aboriginal Men of High Degree*, pp. 129–30). The Mulukmuluk neophyte is attacked by "devils": they kill him, open his abdomen, cook and eat him. "The devils carefully collect the bones into a basket, which two of them rock until the man becomes alive again" (Elkin, *Aboriginal Men of High Degree*, p. 137; on the symbolism of the skeleton and rebirth from the bones, cf. Eliade, *Shamanism*, pp. 158 ff.). Among the Wardoman, the postulant is cut and killed by Wolgara, the spirit who judges the dead. Finally, Wolgara summons a white hawk which reanimates the candidate (Elkin, *Aboriginal Men of High Degree*, p. 137).

takes place as follows. The aspirant enters a cave, and two totemic Heroes (the wildcat and the emu) kill him, open his body, remove the organs, and replace them with magical substances. They also remove the shoulder bone and tibia, which they dry and, before restoring them, stuff with the same substances.[25]

The Aranda know three ways of making medicine men: (1) by the Iruntarinia, or "spirits"; (2) by the Eruncha (i.e., the spirits of the Eruncha men of the mythical times); (3) by other medicine men. In the first case, the candidate goes to sleep in front of the mouth of a cave. An Iruntarinia comes and "throws an invisible lance at him, which pierces the neck from behind, passes through the tongue, making therein a large hole, and then comes out through the mouth." The candidate's tongue remains perforated; one can easily put one's little finger through it. A second lance cuts off his head, and the victim succumbs. One of the Iruntarinia carries him into the cave, which is said to be very deep and where it is believed that these spirits live in perpetual light near cool springs (in fact, the cave represents the Aranda paradise). There this one Iruntarinia tears out his internal organs and gives him others, which are completely new. The candidate returns to life, but for some time behaves like a lunatic.[26] The Iruntarinia then

[25] Elkin, *Aboriginal Men of High Degree*, p. 116; Eliade, *Birth and Rebirth*, p. 97.

[26] The "madness" of the future shaman is a well-known motif in Siberian shamanism but is found also in other parts of the world (cf. Eliade, *Shamanism*, pp. 23 ff., 33 ff., 38 ff., etc.). Though not common in Australia, the motif is attested not only among the Aranda (cf. also Strehlow, quoted by Elkin, *Aboriginal Men of High Degree*, p. 123) but equally among the Pita-Pita (Roth, quoted by Elkin, p. 128) and in eastern Kimberley (Elkin, pp. 138 ff.).

carries him to his camp, although unseen, for such spirits are invisible to all human beings except medicine men. Etiquette forbids the newly made doctor to practice for a year; if during that time the opening in his tongue closes, the candidate gives up, for his mystical virtues are held to have disappeared. During this year he learns the secrets of the profession from other medicine men, especially the use of the quartz stones that the Iruntarinia placed in his body.[27]

The second way of making a medicine man resembles the first, except that, instead of carrying the candidate into a cave, the Eruncha take him underground with them. Finally, the third method involves a long ritual in a solitary place, where the postulant must silently submit to an operation performed by two old medicine men. They rub his body with rock crystals to the point of abrading the skin, press rock crystals into his scalp, pierce a hole under a fingernail of his right hand, and make an incision in his tongue. Finally his forehead is marked with a design called *erunchilda*, literally, "the devil's hand." His body is decorated with another design with a black line in the center representing Eruncha and lines around it apparently symbolizing the magical crystals in his body.[28]

A famous medicine man of the Unmatjera tribe told Spencer and Gillen of the essential moments of his initiation. One day an old doctor "killed" him by throwing crystals (*atnongara* stones) at him with a spear thrower.

[27] Spencer and Gillen, *Native Tribes*, pp. 522 ff.; *idem, The Arunta: A Study of a Stone Age People*, II, 391 ff.; cf. Eliade, *Shamanism*, pp. 46–47.

[28] Spencer and Gillen, *Native Tribes*, pp. 526 ff.; *The Arunta*, II, 394 ff.; Eliade, *Shamanism*, p. 47.

The old man then cut out all of his insides, intestines, liver, heart, lungs—everything in fact, and left him lying all night long on the ground. In the morning the old man came and looked at him and placed some more *atnongara* stones inside his body and in his arms and legs, and covered over his face with leaves. Then he sung over him until his body was swollen up. When this was so he provided him with a complete set of new inside parts, placed a lot more *atnongara* stones in him, and patted him on the head, which caused him to jump up alive.[29]

Among the Warramunga, initiation is performed by the *puntidir* spirits, which are equivalent to the Iruntarinia of the Aranda. A medicine man told Spencer and Gillen that these spirits came and killed him. "While he was lying dead they cut him open and took all his insides out, providing him, however, with a new set, and, finally, they put a little snake inside his body, which endowed him with the powers of a medicine man."[30]

The Binbinga hold that medicine men are consecrated by the spirits Mundadji and Munkaninji (father and son). A doctor, Kurkutji, told how, when entering a cave one day, he came upon the old Mundadji, who caught him by the neck and killed him. He cut him open, "right down the middle line, took out all of his insides and exchanged them for those of himself, which he placed in the body of Kurkutji. At the same time he put a number of sacred stones in his body." After it was all over, Munkaninji, the

[29] Spencer and Gillen, *The Northern Tribes of Central Australia*, pp. 480–81; Eliade, *Shamanism*, pp. 47–48.

[30] Spencer and Gillen, *Northern Tribes*, p. 484; cf. *ibid.*, p. 486, on a second initiation of the Warramunga medicine man; see also Eliade, *Shamanism*, p. 48.

younger spirit, restored him to life and told him he was now a medicine man. Then he took him into the sky and brought him down to earth near his camp, "where he heard the natives mourning for him, thinking that he was dead. For a long time he remained in a more or less dazed condition, but gradually he recovered and the natives knew that he had been made into a medicine man."[31]

In the Mara tribe the technique is almost exactly the same. One who wishes to become a medicine man lights a fire and burns fat, thus attracting two spirits called Minnungara. The spirits first make him insensible, then cut him open and take out all his organs, which they replace by organs from one of their own bodies. Then they bring him to life again and carry him up into the sky. From then on, the Mara medicine man can climb at nighttime by means of a rope into the sky, where he can converse with the star people.[32]

Australian Shamanic Initiations

The characteristic elements of these initiations are (1) the "killing" of the neophyte, (2) the removal of organs and bones and their replacement with new sets, and (3) the insertion of magical substances, especially quartz crystals. A similar pattern is found in the shamanic initiation of central Asia and Siberia, South America, and some parts of Melanesia and Indonesia. The central Asian and Siberian scenarios in particular present the most striking parallels to the examples quoted above. Like the Australian aspirant,

---

[31] Spencer and Gillen, *Northern Tribes*, pp. 487–88.
[32] *Ibid.*, p. 488; Eliade, *Shamanism*, pp. 49–50.

the Siberian and central Asian shaman undergoes an ecstatic initiation during a period of sickness, mental disturbances, or "dream." He sees himself tortured and eventually "killed" by spirits or mythical Heroes. These demonic beings chop his body, disjoint the limbs, cut off the head, boil the flesh, clean the bones, scrape the flesh and replace it with new flesh, and change the body fluids.[33] The motif of inserting magical substances is less frequent; there are only rare references to pieces of iron set to melt in the same caldron with future shaman's flesh and bones.[34] But this motif is attested, for example, among the Semang of the Malay Peninsula,[35] the Dyak of Borneo,[36] and it is a specific trait of South American shamanism.[37]

As we have already pointed out,[38] Elkin compares the initiation pattern of the Australian medicine men to a mummification ritual of eastern Australia, which seems to have been introduced by way of the Torres Strait Islands, where a certain type of mummification was practiced until quite recently. Moreover, Elkin is inclined to relate such Melanesian influences to other higher cultures (Egypt?). We

[33] Cf. Eliade, *Shamanism*, pp. 35 ff.

[34] *Ibid.*, pp. 35, 50, etc. There are other differences: in Siberia the majority of the shamans are "chosen" by spirits or Supernatural Beings; also, their ecstatic experiences are far more "dramatic" (or at least they are described to be so) than among the Australian medicine men.

[35] Spirits and masters of initiation introduce crystals into the candidate's body; cf. Eliade, *Shamanism*, p. 52.

[36] The old shaman inserts magical "power" in the form of pebbles or other objects (*ibid.*, p. 57).

[37] Cf. *ibid.*, pp. 52 ff., etc.

[38] Cf. above, pp. 27 ff., n. 45, referring to Elkin, *Aboriginal Men of High Degree*, pp. 40–41.

shall not discuss here the origin and diffusion of this shamanic initiatory pattern. But the dependence of its Australian variant on a (ultimately Egyptian?) mummification ritual is a gratuitous hypothesis. Are we then to explain the Siberian and South American shamanic initiations by similar influences of mummification rituals? The wide distribution of some complementary initiatory motifs, attested in Siberia as well as in Australia—for instance, the novice's voyages to heaven and into the underground—and also the similarities noticed among shamanistic practices all over the world, point to an archaic stage out of which the different types of shamanism have eventually evolved.

Of course, this does not mean that certain forms of shamanism have not been, in the course of time, strongly influenced by higher and more recent cultures. Central Asian and Siberian shamanism, for instance, presents evident traces of Iranian (ultimately Mesopotamian), Indian, and Buddhist influences.[39] A priori, the possibility of Asian influences on Australian mystical techniques cannot be excluded. Elkin compares the parapsychological powers of the Australian medicine men with the feats of Indian and Tibetan yogis. For walking on fire, using the "magic cord," the power of disappearing and reappearing, "fast traveling," and so on, are just as popular among Australian medicine men as they are among yogis and fakirs. "It is possible," Elkin writes, "that there is some historical connection between the Yoga and occult practices of India and Tibet and the practices and psychic powers of aboriginal men of high degree. Hinduism spread to the East Indies. Yoga is a cult in Bali, and some of the remarkable feats of the Aus-

[39] Cf. Eliade, *Shamanism*, pp. 495 ff.

tralian medicine men are paralleled by their fellow-professionals in Papua."[40]

If Elkin's conjecture should prove correct, we should have, in Australia, a situation comparable to that of central Asia and Siberia. But, again, this does not mean that the corpus of rites, beliefs, and occult techniques of the Australian medicine men was *created* under Indian influence. The archaic structure of most of these rituals and beliefs is obvious. Furthermore, the Australian medicine man stands in the center of the most secret, that is, the *oldest*, religious tradition of his tribe. His "magical tricks" are of an archaic type, and most of them are practiced by the shamans and magicians of other primitive cultures, where it is difficult to assume Indian influences (e.g., the Arctic zones and Tierra del Fuego).[41]

We shall content ourselves with only a brief presentation of one of these "tricks," namely, the "magical rope."[42] We have quoted the example of the Wiradjuri medicine man using a mysterious cord to climb up to heaven (see p. 132).

[40] Elkin, *Aboriginal Men of High Degree*, pp. 76–77. I have already quoted and discussed this passage in *Birth and Rebirth*, p. 100.

[41] On the contrary, as I have already pointed out (p. 28, n. 45), there are notable similarities between the medical ideas and practices of the Australian medicine men and those of the aboriginal tribes of India.

[42] I have discussed this problem in "Mythes et symboles de la corde," *Eranos-Jahrbuch*, XXIX (1961) 109–37, reprinted in my *Mephistophélès et l'androgyne* (Paris, 1962), pp. 200–237 (= "Cordes et marionnettes"). Unfortunately, in the English translation, *Mephistopheles and the Androgyne* (New York, 1965, pp. 160–88), the English quotations are not always reproduced from the original texts, but rendered from the French translation.

According to the information gathered by Berndt, the cord was given by Baiame and "sung" by him into the body of the novice (p. 135). At initiations or before an assembly of fully initiated men, the doctors displayed their powers by "singing out" their cord; lying on their backs under a tree they sent up the cord "in the same manner as does a spider, and began climbing up, using both hands one after the other, so that the top of the tree was reached." They then sent out the cords to the next tree "and walked across through the air."[43]

A magical performance, witnessed by a Wiradjuri during his initiation in about 1882, included walking on fire and climbing up on the magic cord. At that occasion, a Wongai-bon "clever man" lay down on his back near the base of a tree and "sang" his cord out; the cord went directly upward, and he climbed it reaching the top of the tree where there was a nest some forty feet from the ground. "While climbing he was in exactly the same position—head well back, body outstretched, legs apart and arms to the side— as when he 'sang out' his cord. He climbed into the nest, and sat there, waving his hands to the people down below. Then he came down, in the same way that a spider uses its thread, with his back to the ground. When he rested on the ground, the cord could be seen coming down and re-entering the testes."[44]

Similar "tricks" are known also from other primitive societies. For example, the shaman of the Ona, one of the tribes of Tierra del Fuego, possesses a "magic rope" nearly

[43] Berndt, "Wuradjeri Magic," Part I, p. 340.
[44] *Ibid.*, pp. 341–42. Elkin quoted these examples, from Berndt's field notes, in *Aboriginal Men of High Degree*, pp. 64–65.

three meters long, which he produces from his mouth and causes to disappear instantly by swallowing it.[45] As we argued in a previous study, such magical exploits must be compared to the fakirs' "rope trick." Indeed, the two constitutive elements of the rope trick, namely, the climbing of a rope by the conjurer assistant and the dismemberment of his body, are to be found conjointly in the traditions of Australian medicine men. The significance of these exploits is obvious: they illustrate the occult power of the medicine men, their ability to transcend "this world" and act like Supernatural Beings and mythical Heroes. Climbing to the top of trees on the "magic cord" is a "proof" of the medicine man's capability to ascend to heaven and meet the celestial High Beings.

Medicine Men and the Rainbow Serpent

The insertion of quartz crystals or other magical substances (pearl shells or "spirit snakes") into the body of the future medicine man seems to be a pan-Australian practice. The possession of such substances is "absolutely essential, for the medicine man's powers are associated with, and indeed mediated through, them."[46] As a matter of fact, the assimilation of such substances is tantamount to a mystical "transmutation" of the medicine man's body. Among some southeastern tribes the quartz crystals are supposed to have fallen from the vault of heaven. They are in a sense "solidified light."[47] But almost everywhere in southeast and

[45] See E. Lucas Bridges, *The Uttermost Part of the Earth* (New York, 1948) pp. 284 ff.

[46] Elkin, *The Australian Aborigines*, p. 304.

[47] Eliade, *Mephistophélès et l'androgyne*, pp. 24 ff. The old sources on the quartz crystals are compiled and discussed by Mauss, "L'Origine des pouvoirs magiques," pp. 136, n. 1; 137, n. 3; 139 ff.

northwest Australia the quartz is connected with the sky
world and with the rainbow.[48] Pearl shells are similarly
connected with the Rainbow Serpent, that is, in fact, both
with the sky and with the waters. To possess such substances in his own body ultimately means to partake of the
mystical essence of the celestial High Beings or of the cosmic deity par excellence, the Rainbow Serpent.

Indeed, in a great number of tribes the medicine men are
reputed to obtain their powers from the Rainbow Snake.[49]
According to an early account, the Brisbane natives believed that quartz crystals were vomited by the Rainbow
Snake: "the medicine men knew where to dive for them,
i.e., wherever the rainbow ended."[50] The medicine men of
the Kabi, a tribe in Queensland, receive from the Rainbow
Snake not only the crystals but also the "magical cord."[51]
Mathews reported that a Wiradjuri doctor can go and
meet the Serpent Wāwi, "who conducts him into his den
and sings him a new song for the corroboree." The doctor
rehearses until he learns the song, then he returns and

[48] See Elkin, *Aboriginal Men of High Degree,* pp. 43 ff.; cf. also
pp. 93, 98, 103, and 107 ff. on the role of quartz crystals in the
making of medicine men.

[49] A. R. Radcliffe Brown, "The Rainbow-Serpent Myth of Aus-
tralia," *Journal of the Royal Anthropological Institute,* LVI (1926),
19–25, esp. p. 19 (Queensland) and p. 24 (Kakadu, in Northern
Territory); *idem,* "The Rainbow-Serpent Myth in South-East
Australia," *Oceania,* I (1930), 342–47; A. P. Elkin, "The Rainbow-
Serpent in North-West Australia," *Oceania,* I (1930), 349–52
(Forest River District, Karadjeri, etc.); *idem, Aboriginal Men of
High Degree,* p. 144; etc.

[50] Radcliffe-Brown, "The Rainbow-Serpent Myth of Australia,"
p. 20; cf. above n. 22.

[51] J. Mathews quoted by Radcliffe-Brown, "The Rainbow-Serpent Myth of Australia," pp. 20–21.

teaches his fellows to sing and dance.[52] Among the tribes Lunga and Djara, in Hall's Creek District, the medicine man is made by Kulabel, the Rainbow Snake, who "kills" the aspirant when he is bathing at a water hole. He becomes sick and mad, but eventually he receives his power, which is associated with quartz crystals.[53] For the Unambal, the source of the medicine man's power is Ungud. During his sleep, the aspirant's soul goes to Ungud, and he receives crystals from the subterranean Snake.[54] Also among the Ungarinyin the vocation and power of the medicine man are provoked and bestowed by Ungud, and in a few cases by the Celestial Hero Wálangala.[55]

Functions and Prestiges of the Medicine Men

We see now that the initiation achieves the "transmutation" of the aspirant's human condition. He "dies" and has his bones and flesh cleaned or replaced and his body stuffed with magical substances; he flies to heaven, dives in the waters, or goes underground to meet Supernatural Beings, Ancestral Heroes, or ghosts; and finally he comes back to life—a radically "changed" being. As a matter of fact, he is now, ontologically as well as existentially, nearer to the Primordial Beings than to his own human fellows. Not only can he see, meet, and converse with such Beings, generally invisible or inaccessible to ordinary mortals, but he behaves

[52] Radcliffe-Brown, "The Rainbow-Serpent Myth of Australia," p. 21.

[53] Elkin, "The Rainbow-Serpent in North-West Australia," p. 350; *idem, Aboriginal Men of High Degree*, pp. 138 ff.

[54] A. Lommel, *Die Unambal: Ein Stamm in Nordwest-Australien* (Hamburg, 1952), pp. 42 ff.

[55] H. Petri, *Sterbende Welt in Nordwest-Australien* (Braunschweig, 1954), pp. 250 ff.

like one of them, and precisely the one who initiated him or
gave him his mysterious, superhuman powers. Like the
Primordial Beings, the medicine man can now fly, disappear
and reappear, see the spirits of the living and the dead, etc.

Thanks to his "transmutation," the medicine man lives
simultaneously in two worlds: in his actual tribal world
and in the sacred world of the beginning, when the Primordial Beings were present and active on earth. For this
reason the medicine man constitutes the intermediary par
excellence between his tribe and the Heroes of his tribe's
mythical history. More and better than other members of
the tribe, he can reactivate the contact with the Dreaming
Time and thus renew his world. And because he can reintegrate at will the fabulous epoch of the beginnings, he
can "dream" new myths and rituals. Such new creations are
eventually introduced into the religious tradition of the
tribe, but without bearing the mark of personal innovation,
for they belong to the same primordial, eternal source of
the Dreaming Time.

All the public functions and duties of the medicine man
are justified by his singular existential condition. He can
cure the sick because he can see the magical objects that
caused a sickness, and he can eliminate or annihilate them.[56]
He can be a rainmaker because he is able to go to heaven or
summon the clouds.[57] And when he defends his tribe
against magical aggression, the medicine man acts as a black
magician: no one can use the "pointing bone" better than
he or surpass him in "singing" a deadly poison into a vic-

[56] See the bibliography in Petri, "Der australische Medizinmann,"
Part II, p. 160, n. 238. Cf. also Lommel, *Die Unambal*, pp. 45 ff.
[57] See Petri, "Der australische Medizinmann," Part II, pp. 175–90;
idem, Sterbende Welt, pp. 175–90.

tim. His social prestige, his cultural role, and his political supremacy derive ultimately from his magico-religious "power." Among the Wiradjuri it was believed that a very powerful doctor was capable even of reviving a dead man.[58] Summarizing the role of the Wiradjuri medicine man, Berndt emphasizes his "deep knowledge of all tribal matters, particularly those relating to the traditional and religious life." He was par excellence the "intellectual" of the tribe, and at the same time a man of great social prestige. "It was possible for him to assume the chief headmanship and to play a leading part in the totemic ceremonial life; in this way he could become both temporal and spiritual leader of the group."[59]

But, although enjoying a singularly privileged position, the medicine man is not the only one capable of re-establishing contact with the Heroes of the primordial times, and thus gaining magico-religious powers. As a matter of fact, every fully initiated member of the tribe can, through specific rituals, reintegrate the mythical epoch. The "increase ceremonies," for instance, or the ritual repainting of the Wondjina images, are periodically performed by a variety of initiated adults. Every one re-enacts, and thus relives, his particular sacred "history." Moreover, there are specific magical powers which can be, at least in part, mastered by any adult male. Anyone can practice black magic by "singing" or by the "pointing bone."[60] Likewise,

[58] But only if the deceased too were a "strong man"; Berndt, "Wuradjeri Magic," Part II, pp. 82 ff.

[59] *Ibid.*, Part I, p. 332.

[60] Petri, "Der australische Medizinmann," Part II, pp. 160 ff.; cf. p. 164, n. 234, a bibliography on "black magic." See also R. M. and C. H. Berndt, *The World of the First Australians* (Chicago, 1965), pp. 266 ff.

rainmaking is not an exclusive privilege of the medicine man. There are professional rainmakers, and, furthermore, there are many other inspired individuals who can produce rain.[61]

Yet there still are other types of magicians and ecstatics whose functions, in some cases, overlap with those of the medicine man. As we have already seen, the doctor can fight the black magician with the latter's very own techniques. With few exceptions, found mainly in the southeast part of the continent, the medicine man does not practice black magic for aggressive purposes and personal reasons; and in the exceptional cases when he resorts to it, it is against members of other, hostile tribes. The antisocial drives of the sorceror and black magician singularize them, and distinguish them as clearly as possible from the medicine man.

Such differences are less evident, however, between the medicine man and the so-called "corroboree doctor," the inventor of new songs and dances. Certainly any medicine man can invent new corroborees as a result of oneiric or ecstatic experiences. In a great number of tribes, the medicine men are inspired by their voyages to and into the land of spirits, and consequently the enrichment of the tribal tradition is achieved through these tribally recognized spiritual guides.[62] For instance, among the Kulin, the Wotjobaluk, and the Wurunjeri, the medicine men are also the bards of the tribe, and in some cases the bard's

[61] In central Kimberley, though each chief of a totemic group can produce the rain by repainting a particular Wondjina, only the medicine man is capable of stopping the rain; cf. Petri, "Der australische Medizinmann," Part II, p. 187.

[62] See the examples listed in *ibid.*, pp. 192 ff.

direct inspiration comes from Bunjil.[63] But, as we have
seen (p. 137, above), the Kurnai distinguish between the
true medicine man (*mulla-mullung*) and the visionary poet
and creator of corroborees, *birra-ark*. Among some tribes,
the authors of new songs and dances are classified as a
special group. In western Kimberley, for example, the invention of new corroborees is a part of the medicine man's
function, while in central Kimberley the so-called "Devil
doctor" is clearly distinguished from the "Ungud doctor."
The "Devil doctor" divulges new corroborees following
his ecstatic (i.e., oneiric) voyages in the land of the dead
or his encounter with bush spirits, while the source of inspiration of the other class of doctors is Ungud.[64]

Ultimately, the dichotomy between medicine man and
"corroboree doctor" may have its origin in the increasing
religious importance of a certain type of ecstatic experience, namely, the voyage in the land of the spirits and of
the dead. The creation of new songs and dances has become
more and more dependent on such types of personal, spontaneous, ecstatic experience. Thus religious and artistic
creativity was encouraged among individuals outside of the
traditional closed group of professionals.

[63] Howitt, *The Native Tribes of South-East Australia*, p. 418.
[64] Petri, "Der australische Medizinmann," Part II, pp. 90 ff. There
are also examples of songs and dances inspired directly by a spirit.
This is the case among the Dieiri: when a man dies, the spirit
appears to his younger brother and, during several nights, teaches
him a new chant; cf. O. Siebert, "Sagen und Sitten der Dieiri und
Nachbar-Stämme in Zentral-Australien," *Globus*, XCVII (1910),
185. Exceptionally, as among the Barkinji of the Darling River, the
experts in black magic are equally the authors of new corroborees;
cf. F. Bonney (1884), quoted by Petri, "Der australische Medizinmann," Part II, p. 193.

"Specialists" and "Innovators"

We are confronted with two different, though somehow related, categories of religious phenomena: (1) the consequences deriving from the variety of the medicine man's magico-religious experiences and (2) the tendency of the nonprofessionals to enlarge their "powers" and socio-religious prestige by acquiring some of the professional's esoteric knowledge and secret techniques.

The medicine man's various activities are fostered by the many different possibilities he has to experiment with the sacred and master the magico-religious forces. Like the shamans and other religious professionals, the Australian medicine man is a "specialist of the sacred." But the great variety of his experiences with the sacred invites further "specialization"; thus, as we have just seen, at a certain moment and among certain tribes the rainmaker or the ecstatic author of new songs and dances becomes part of a new class. It is difficult to decide whether the process of "specialization" has always started within a class of medicine men in which all these functions coexisted or, on the contrary, whether the "specialization" has taken place among spiritually gifted individuals outside the professional group. Most probably it has happened in both ways—for, as we have seen, a medicine man can be, and often is, also a rainmaker, a poet, and author of new corroborees, whereas, vice versa, any initiated male may acquire one of these techniques and become a "specialist." But a rainmaker as such can never fulfill the complex functions of the traditional medicine man or enjoy his religious and social prestige. And it is probable that at a certain moment the same could have been said with regard to those authors of corroborees who were outside the professional group.

As regards the tendency of the nonprofessional to acquire magico-religious powers through the "specialist's" techniques, this is a well-known and universal phenomenon. In Australia, such a tendency is validated and encouraged by the tribal initiation. A fully initiated male is not only introduced to the sacred history of his tribe but also taught how to recapture the sacredness of the fabulous beginnings. In some cases—in Kimberley and elsewhere—the very introduction of an individual into the religious life confers upon him one of the medicine man's powers, namely, the power to bring the rain.

In general, one could say that two ways lie open to a nonprofessional desiring to augment his magico-religious powers: (1) the techniques of black magic and (2) ecstatic experiences. The most elementary black magic, that is, the "pointed bone," is accessible to everyone; but more complicated acts (e.g., "fat stealing") are restricted to the "specialist." Moreover, the fear of black magic and, consequently, the risk of being suspected of sorcery, is so widespread that very few might be tempted to increase their powers by acquiring such dangerous techniques.

On the contrary, the oneiric and ecstatic experiences represent the source of magico-religious powers par excellence. Here also the traditional medicine man served as a model. But the ecstatic-oneiric experiences of the nonprofessionals were less rigidly dependent on archaic patterns, and hence their religious and artistic expressions could make, in some cases, a deeper impression on some sections of the tribe. On the other hand, lacking the well-articulated esoteric mythology of the medicine man, the ecstatic's creations could be appropriated, modified, and used for various purposes. In some cases, the corroboree became a magically oriented ritual, though not necessarily of the "black magic" type. But in the process of acculturation, under the impact of Western Culture, some of the new corroborees became independent wandering cults. The original intention of the corroboree, namely, the nonprofessional's desire to augment his magico-religious powers, gave place to an antitraditional and aggressive attitude. Thus the new corroborees express both a rebellion against the traditional religious system of the tribe, represented chiefly by the medicine men, and a public avowal of the growing interest in magical powers as such. As we shall see in the next chapter, the Kuràngara cult abundantly illustrates such a process.

In sum, *the imitation of the Supernatural Beings, revealed and taught to the medicine man during his initiation, is repeated, at another, lower level, by the spontaneous or voluntary imitation of the medicine man's own techniques by nonprofessional but gifted individuals.* A similar situation is found in other parts of the world. In some parts of Siberia and Oceania, the shaman's behavior, techniques, and trances are imitated or feigned by all kinds of ecstatic or psychotic individuals, and even by children.[65] Ultimately, such phenomena illustrate the desires and hopes of the nonprofessionals to acquire the "power" and prestige of the "specialists of the sacred" without, however, submitting themselves to the hardships, risks, suffering, and long period of learning demanded by the traditional initiation of "men of high degree." From a certain point of view one may

[65] See some examples in Eliade, *Shamanism*, pp. 252 ff. (Koryak, Chukchee) and pp. 362 ff. (Oceania).

identify in this process the beginnings of "secularization," for it clearly expresses the reaction against the privileged religious elite, and, implicitly, the will to empty that elite's values, behavior, and institutions of the sacred aura they originally had. On the other hand, the secularization of a traditional religious form opens the way to a process of re-sacralization of other sectors of the collective or individual life.

CHAPTER 5

Death and Eschatology: Conclusions

Death, Funerary Rites, and "Inquest"

The medicine man plays a central role in death rituals, for he is able to discover the "murderer" and thus to direct the revenge. Thanks to his spiritual powers and social prestige, the crisis provoked by death does not materialize in frantic suicidal actions. As in so many other religions, the very act of dying is evaluated in terms that contradict each other. On the one hand, the Australians believe that only through death does man reach his highest spiritual status, that is, he becomes a purely spiritual being. "Death, the final rite of passage, transfers him from all the world of the profane and puts him (his soul) entirely into the world of the sacred."[1] On the other hand, with very few exceptions (e.g., infants or the very old men), every new death occasions a catastrophic crisis. The entire community reacts with its utmost energy and after completing the first funerary rites burns down the property of the deceased and abandons the camp. Like birth, death is not "natural"; it is provoked by someone. All dead are victims of sorcery. The magic accounts even for such emphatically "natural" causes as being speared in combat; for, it is argued, the blow was fatal only because a sorcerer made it so. With every new

---

[1] Warner, *A Black Civilization*, p. 402.

death, the society in its totality relives the same dark menace perceived for the first time when death made its appearance in the world. For death was not unavoidable. Men are mortal because the mythical Ancestor was killed or because he was prevented from coming back to life. The absurdity of dying is proclaimed with every new death: it is not a "natural" event, it is a murder effectuated by spiritual means, that is, by magic. Consequently, the criminal has to be sought out and discovered and the victim avenged.

In some parts of the continent, during his death agony, the relatives gather around a man and chant songs of his totemic cult clan. This comforts the dying man and prepares him for the return to the sacred spirit world. As long as he can, he takes part in the singing.[2] Among the Murngin, the song summons his father and his ancestors. "If we didn't sing he might go back because evil ghosts (*mokois*) might catch him and take him out in the jungle country where they live. It is better that his old grandfathers and his ancestors come and get him and take him straight to his clan well where his totem came from" (Warner, *A Black Civilization*, p. 403).

Every man has two souls: the real self—"the eternal dream-time soul which pre-existed and will exist, for a time or eternally, and which in some tribes, may be reincarnated" —and another soul, "which can appear in dreams, which may take up its abode within another person after its owner's death, or may live in the bush and play tricks, scare and even damage its incarnate relations" (Elkin, *The Australian Aborigines*, p. 317). It is this second soul, the trickster,

---

[2] Elkin, *The Australian Aborigines*, p. 315; Warner, *A Black Civilization*, pp. 403 ff.

which resists the definitive separation from the body, and it is especially against it that the living defend themselves with the help of rituals.

The wailing of women, the gashing on the head to draw blood, and other manifestations of grief and despair begin during the agony, but they reach a real frenzy immediately after death. Menaces are uttered against those who could have protected the victims from the black magic but failed to do so. The collective grief and wrath are controlled only by the certainty and the emphatic reassurance that the dead will be avenged. The victim himself will help to identify his murderer. For, although there are many kinds of inquests, almost all of them are directed either by the indication given by the corpse or by the soul using its former body to inform the medicine men. There are different types of burial, among the most common being interment, cremation, and exposition of the body on a platform[3]—but none is immediate and radical. Usually there are two or three stages between the "official" declaration of death and the definitive abandonment of the remains, and the "inquest" takes place during one of these stages. The medicine man can discover the country of the murderer by examining the ground around the grave, or by seeing the spirit of the dead coming out of the grave on the side nearest the murderer's country, or by perceiving the spirit of the culprit near the grave, or else by dreaming of him.[4]

[3] On the different types of burial, see Elkin, *The Australian Aborigines*, pp. 329 ff.; R. M. and C. H. Berndt, *The World of the First Australians*, pp. 329 ff.

[4] On the inquest, cf. Elkin, *The Australian Aborigines*, pp. 311 ff.; R. M. and C. H. Berndt, *The World of the First Australians*, pp. 406 ff.; Helmut Petri, "Der australische Medizinma in," Part II, *Annali Lateranensi* (Città del Vaticano), XVII (1953), 170 ff.

But the corpse, or rather the spirit which is nearby, is also able to indicate the "murderer." For instance, the dead man's hair is pulled in jerks while names of different tribes are pronounced, and the guilty group is revealed when some hair is removed. In northeastern South Australia the following method was used: the corpse was placed on the heads of three men, and when mention was made of the murderer's tribe, the corpse jumped off. Also, the corpse may be disinterred and the internal organs examined. As Elkin puts it: "The forms of inquest show that the spirit of the deceased still 'animates,' controls or may use the corpse or parts of it. . . . Indeed, it is not until revenge has been taken or satisfaction obtained, and the burial and mourning rites completed, that the spirit finally leaves the body and goes to the home of the dead or its spirit-home" (p. 325). But the very fact of a delayed and prolonged inquest, with the elaborate interpretation of the signs indicating the country and the group of the culprit, limits the gravity of the revenge. As a matter of fact, the revenge expedition is not always organized—"a magical rite may be performed instead, an invitation to a meeting and fight may be set, a settlement may be made by the 'payment' of a woman, the present death may be balanced against a previous death or other grievance which the murderer's group has against the deceased's group, or, as in some tribes, the initiation, that is a ritual killing of a young member of the former group, may satisfy the latter" (p. 328).

The Postexistence of the Soul

The inquest and the burial rites help us to understand the Australian ideas of the soul. As everywhere else, the conception of the soul and its postexistence are confusing and not seldom contradictory. As we have seen already, there are two souls, and only the "primary pre-existent spirit" is supposed to have a meaningful postexistence. In fact, it returns to its spirit home, from which it came originally or where its creator lives. This home may be the sky (as in most of eastern Australia and parts of the west and northwest) or the totem centers (as in the greatest part of northern and central Australia), or, in some cases, beyond the sea.[5] In the northeastern part of Arnhem Land, it is said that a human spirit divides after death into three parts. "One returns to its totemic center, to wait for rebirth. One, the *mogwoi*, is a trickster spirit which is much more mobile but still remains locality-bound. The third goes to the appropriate land of the dead, to join and then merge with the creative beings and spirits already there."[6]

As we might expect, the land of the dead is differently imagined. At the Australian level of culture we already find the most characteristic traits of what may be called the mythical geography of the disincarnated soul. Thus, the spirits ascend to heaven by a rope thrown by some Supernatural Beings;[7] or they cross an invisible tree which forms a bridge from a rock to the land of the dead, the crossing itself accompanied by several other tests;[8] or, as among the Wiradjuri, the spirits climb a cord up to the sky world of Baiame;[9] or, as among Kulin, they ascend to the sky on the

[5] Cf. Elkin, *The Australian Aborigines*, p. 336; R. M. and C. H. Berndt, *The World of the First Australians*, pp. 412 ff.

[6] R. M. and C. H. Berndt, *The World of the First Australians*, p. 416. The Dieiri too distinguish three souls (*ibid.*, p. 413).

[7] In the Lower Murray River; cf. *ibid.*, p. 412.

[8] This is a well-known and widely distributed motif (cf. Eliade, *Shamanism*, pp. 482 ff.).

[9] R. M. and C. H. Berndt, *The World of the First Australians*, p. 413; A. W. Howitt, *The Native Tribes of South-East Australia*, pp. 435 ff.

"bright rays of the setting sun" (Howitt, pp. 438–39). For the tribes on the Herbert River in northeastern Queensland, the dead travel to the sky by the milky way (p. 431); the Kamilaroi believe that their dead go to the Magellan clouds (p. 439). For the eastern Kimberley tribes, the land of the dead lies in the west. The spirits "occasionally return to their own country, to their graves or to the gorges where their bones have been hidden."[10] The *jiridja* moiety of the tribes in northeastern Arnhem Land believes that the land of the dead consists of certain Torres Straits Islands along with the southern coast of New Guinea; for the *dua* moiety, it is the island of Bralgu. The arriving soul is tested before being accepted, a motif also found elsewhere in Australia. In the case of the *dua* moiety the guardian examines the newcomer to see if he was initiated (R. M. and C. H. Berndt, *The World of the First Australians*, pp. 416 ff.). Among the Gunwinggu of western Arnhem Land, the spirit is helped to pass unobserved by the wife of the guardian of the road (p. 414). And the experiences and initiatory tests of the Wiradjuri medicine man, climbing into the sky world to bring the rain,[11] also confront every soul at death (p. 413).

Death is essentially an ecstatic experience: the soul abandons the body and journeys to the land of its postexistence. The difference from other ecstatic states—sleep, trance provoked by sickness, shamanistic voyages—consists in the fact that the soul of the dead leaves the body for good, thus

[10] Kaberry, quoted in R. M. and C. H. Berndt, *The World of the First Australians*, p. 414. On Melville and Bathurst Islands the spirits "return to the place of their birth at the various totemic sites" (*ibid.*).

[11] Quoted above, p. 134.

bringing on the decay and final destruction of the latter. Howitt quotes a certain number of voyages to heaven accomplished by ordinary people, even women (i.e., non-initiated persons).[12] Such spontaneous ecstatic journeys, however, are rather rare. On the contrary, the medicine men travel frequently to heaven or wherever the land of the dead is situated. And there are even stories of men who visited such fabulous countries *in concreto*. Warner and the Berndts cite the story of a man, Jalngura, who paddled for several days, reached Bralgu, the island of the dead, where he met different spirits and finally came back to his village, but died that very night.[13]

All these journeys to the land of the dead have a prototype: the first voyage of the Supernatural Beings or of the mythical Ancestors. In southeast Australia the Supernatural Beings retired to heaven, and likewise, at the end of their cultural activity, some of the *mura-mura* climbed there too.[14] The medicine men repeat this celestial ascent, and so does the soul of every man after death. Once again, though for the last time, *man does what was done in the beginning by a Supernatural Being*. With every new death, the primordial scenario is re-enacted. No moral issues are involved in successfully reaching the abode of the dead and joining the other spirits. There is no punishment for sins, and the only tests are of an initiatory character. If there is a discrimination between the souls, implying differences in their postmortem condition, it is in relation to the rituals performed and the religious knowledge received and assimi-

---

[12] Howitt, *The Native Tribes of South-East Australia*, pp. 436 ff.
[13] R. M. and C. H. Berndt, *The World of the First Australians*, pp. 417–18.
[14] Howitt, *The Native Tribes of South-East Australia*, pp. 426 ff.

lated during the lifetime, that is to say, in the degree of their initiation. One of the characteristics of archaic conceptions of death and postmortem existence is such an indifference to "moral" values. It seems as if, in this perspective, "morality" is meaningful exclusively for man in the incarnate condition but is insignificant in the postmortem state, which is a purely "spiritual" mode of being. Such "spiritual" existences are susceptible to modification primarily by the force of the rituals performed and by the "saving knowledge" accumulated on earth.

But whatever may be the nature or the proportion of the postmortem modifications, the indestructibility of the human spirit seems to be a fundamental and pan-Australian conception.[15] Essentially this means the indestructibility of the spiritual unit which made its appearance in the Dreaming Time. We may compare this conception with the pre-systematic ideas of *karma* and the permanence of *ātman*. In post-Vedic India, as well as in Australia, the rituals—that is, the repetition of paradigmatic acts—and the "saving knowledge" derived from the understanding of the divine origin and essence of the rituals led to the idea of an indestructible spiritual agent.

Kuràngara

We have previously discussed some new religious creations, occasioned by contact with Melanesian culture (see above, p. 150). In recent times, the impact of Western civilization provoked still more radical reactions. A case in point is the Kuràngara, a cult which originated in the cen-

[15] "Despite occasional remarks to the contrary, there seems to be some agreement on the indestructibility of the human spirit" (R. M. and C. H. Berndt, *The World of the First Australians*, p. 419).

tral desert, probably no more than sixty to seventy years ago, and spread with great rapidity to the north and north-west.[16] Its interest for the historian of religions is its rejection of the traditional religious behavior and ideology, and the exaltation of magical power. The Kuràngara does not everywhere present the same mythico-ritual scenario. In 1938, Helmut Petri investigated the cult among the Ungarinyin, where it was in full development, and Andreas Lommel among the Unambal, where it was in its initial phase. Already at that time the differences were notable.[17] When, in 1944–45, Ronald Berndt studied the Kuràngara (*gu'rangara*) in the upper Kimberleys, he found a quite different situation; not only were its original function and meaning changed, but in those regions the *gu'rangara* was integrated in the Kalwadi-Kadjari-Kunapipi cult, that is to say, in a "fertility" complex.[18]

As far as we can judge from the information available, the meaning and function of Kuràngara can be best grasped among the Ungarinyin. There, the cult reveals a brutal reaction against the traditional religious values of the old

[16] Helmut Petri, "Kuràngara. Neue magische Kulte in Nordwest-Australien," *Zeitschrift für Ethnologie*, LXXV (1950), 43–51, esp. 50; *idem, Sterbende Welt in Nordwest-Australien* (Braunschweig, 1954), p. 263; *idem*, "Wandlungen in der geistigen Kultur nordwestaustralicher Stämme," *Veröffentlichungen aus dem Museum für Natur-, Völker- und Handelskunde in Bremen*, Ser. B., No. 1 (1950), pp. 33–121, esp. 90 ff. Cf. also E. Worms, "Die Goranara—Feier in australischen Kimberley," *Annali Lateranensi*, VI (1942), 208–35.

[17] Andreas Lommel, "Modern Culture Influences on the Aborigines," *Oceania*, XXI (1950–51), 14–24, esp. p. 22; *idem, Die Unambal* (Hamburg, 1952), pp. 82 ff.

[18] Ronald M. Berndt, "Influence of European Culture on Australian Aborigines," *Oceania*, XXI (1950–51), 229–40, esp. 233.

generation, and a trust in the "saving power" of a new type of secret society. According to Petri, the root of the term Kuràngara is unknown, but the natives translate this word by "poison," meaning that it is magically powerful and dangerous.[19] The central figures of the cult are the Djanba, who may be classified as anthropomorphous spirits, but skeleton-like and tall as trees, with long sexual organs. They are cannibals and can disappear or take any form. The Djanba are invisible to noninitiates. They are considered immortal: they came into being at the beginning of time; "they made themselves." Petri compares them to Ungud (*Sterbende Welt*, p. 258). Their power is due to a magical substance, *gróare*, which they have in their bodies.[20] Because of this *gróare*, the Djanba can see everything that is hidden.

The most important sacred object of the cult is a wooden slab called *minboru*, similar to the central Australian *tjurunga*, but sometimes up to two meters long. The *minboru* are deposited in the secret places where the Kuràngara is carried out. They are said to have originated from the bodies of the Djanba and are the visible representatives of them. In central Kimberley only those who have already gone through tribal initiation can become members of

[19] Petri, "Kuràngara," p. 43. In his book, *Sterbende Welt in Nordwest-Australien*, p. 257, Petri remarks that among the western and southwestern Aranda groups the terms *kuran* and *kuranita* mean "spirit," "shadow," "life-essence," but also "blood." The suffix -*ngara* designates, in Kimberley, "appertaining to." All over Australia the ritual objects of very distant tribes are considered magically powerful. This is, of course, a well-known phenomenon: the "foreigners" are looked upon as magicians, cannibals, or ghosts; their religious activities and objects are considered deadly powerful.

[20] *Gróare* is compared by the initiates to the spirals or concentric circles engraved on the sacred woods, *minboru*.

Kuràngara, but in western Kimberley such conditions are not necessary.[21] The rituals, consisting of corroborees, dances, and bodily painting, re-enact the deeds of the Djanba. Songs are chanted in an unknown language (some words, however, belong to a central Australian dialect).[22] The essential rite consists in eating kangaroo flesh and pressing a *minboru* on the body. Through the ritual, man receives *gróare* and gains power. The chief of the cult, the "Kuràngara doctor," possesses great quantities of *gróare* and as a result has direct rapport with the Djanba; he can see them and converse with them.[23]

Helmut Petri speaks of "black magic."[24] The acculturated young men are impressed with the seemingly unlimited powers of the white men, and they hope to obtain comparable powers through magic. They are convinced that, like the medicine men, they too can project such magical "power" and kill at a distance. They do not believe

[21] Petri, "Kuràngara," p. 47; *idem, Sterbende Welt*, p. 262.

[22] The origin of the belief in Djanba is still an open question. Worms thought that it derived from the cultic system of the Mangala and Walmadjeri, tribes from south of the Fitzroy River (cf. Worms, "Die Goranara"). But Petri rightly observes that, in the *gerangara* of these tribes, Djanba represent a foreign element, brought in from central Australia. Nevertheless, notwithstanding the Aranda origin of some cultic elements, we do not find the cult or the mythology of Kuràngara among the Aranda. (Djanba, for instance, were not noticed.) Petri surmises that Kuràngara might have originated among some of the ethnic groups west of the Aranda, whose culture is today inaccessible (*Sterbende Welt*, p. 261).

[23] Petri, *Sterbende Welt*, p. 259. Kuràngara is the unseen active force of the Djanba, but it is also the "singing," the technique of the black magic; cf. *idem*, "Der australische Medizinmann," Part II, p. 165.

[24] Petri, "Kuràngara," p. 49.

anymore in the values accepted by their forefathers. They look to the Djanba to obtain the powers which, they think, the traditional Supernatural Beings and Cultural Heroes could not give them. As a matter of fact, most Kuràngara members are young men whom the medicine men—the "Ungud doctors"—refused to initiate in the tribal mysteries because they followed "the white man's way." The "Kuràngara doctors" have thus become the competitors of the traditional medicine men.[25] The members of the cult are against the "Ungud doctors" and the elders, keepers of the traditions. They consider the tribal initiation less important than Kuràngara and even negligible; the bull-roarers, sacred for the older generation, are forgotten, their place being taken by the *minboru;* and the Djanba replace the traditional Supernatural Beings.

Notwithstanding all this, we still have here a recent reevaluation of the pan-Australian mythico-ritual pattern. The Djanba were probably a class of Culture Heroes; the Kuràngara ritual seems to be the adaptation of a traditional initiation sequence; the *minboru* slabs are a variant of the central Australian *tjurunga.* The structure of Kuràngara resembles that of any other Australian secret cult: mythical Beings are expected to transmit powers through dances, manipulation of sacred objects, and other specific rituals. What is new is the ideological orientation: the breaking off from the old religious tradition and the exaltation of the magical powers. Being a response to a cultural situation which is becoming rapidly generalized, namely, the situation created by increasing contacts with Western civilization, the diffusion of Kuràngara is remarkably dynamic.

[25] Petri, *Sterbende Welt,* pp. 218 ff., 256.

The overwhelming importance of "magic" is understandable in a popular movement born from a spiritual crisis. The phenomenon, well known throughout the history of religions, was noticed elsewhere in Australia. We have already pointed out how, very recently, a women's secret cult has attracted the younger generation for exclusively magical reasons.[26] The exuberant efflorescence of magical elements in the latest phases of Indian Tantrism represents a similar phenomenon. "Magic" flourishes when the meaning of traditional religious forms is lost or becomes irrelevant. But the essential ritual and ideological elements of the predominant religious system are not abolished; with a degraded or distorted meaning, they are reorganized to serve different purposes. For the younger generation of many Australian tribes, Kuràngara is the only possible answer to the profound crisis caused by the collapse of the traditional values.

It is significant that this new dynamic cult presents the character of a hasty *imitation*. Discussing analogous religious processes in *Patterns in Comparative Religion*, we used the expression *doublets faciles* ("easy substitutes" is only an approximate translation).[27] Indeed, what strikes one in such a development is the *facility* with which certain goals are supposedly attained. In the case of Kuràngara, the "powers" both of the traditional magician and of the white man are proclaimed accessible to *everybody*, without the personal vocation, the training, and the initiation which, up to a few years ago, were considered indispensable.

Among the Unambal the cult, as it was investigated by

[26] Above, pp. 118 ff.
[27] Eliade, *Patterns in Comparative Religion* (New York, 1958), pp. 383 ff., 448.

Lommel in 1938, seems even more strongly influenced by Western symbols and ideology. Tjanba (= Djanba) has a house of corrugated iron and hunts with a rifle. He is able to impart leprosy and syphilis, diseases hitherto unknown. He asks his fellow ghosts for tea, sugar, and bread. "The cult language is pidgin-English. The cult is directed by a 'boss,' the slabs are stored away by a 'clerc,' the feasts are announced by a 'mailman,' and order and discipline during them is maintained by some specially appointed 'pickybas' (from police-boys)." The "boss" uses the same methods as the traditional medicine man, "only the symbols have changed. It is now no longer the Ungud snake but the Kuràngara slab which incorporates life and death."[28]

According to Lommel, the cult expresses the fear of the approaching end of the world. His Unambal informants described the eschatological syndrome in terms familiar to many other traditions: "the social order will be completely reversed: women will take the place of men; they will arrange the feasts and hand on the slabs, whereas the men will gather edible roots, without being allowed to participate in the feasts."[29]

Some of Lommel's interpretations have been challenged by Ronald Berndt, especially the supposed pessimism of the cult and its antifeminism. Berndt demonstrates the integration of Kuràngara in the ritual system of Kunapipi, where women play a role.[30] He also reminds us that in the mythology of the Australian fertility cults the source of ritual

[28] Lommel, "Modern Cultural Influences on the Aborigines," p. 23; cf. *idem, Die Unambal,* pp. 82 ff.
[29] Lommel, "Modern Cultural Influences on the Aborigines," p. 24.
[30] R. M. Berndt, "Influence of European Culture," p. 233.

power and sacredness is found in women.[31] But these inconsistencies and contradictions may be explained by the different re-evaluations of Kuràngara ideology and purposes in the cult's diffusion from tribe to tribe.

Wandering Cults and Millenaristic Movements

Kuràngara is exceptional only because of its amazing vitality, success, and wide diffusion. Many other wandering cults were noticed at the turn of the century.[32] In almost every one of them the "black magic" elements were strongly emphasized.[33] One could describe their emergence and growth in the following terms: a dynamic and magically oriented cult originates from a partial disintegration of the traditional pattern, accompanied by a reorganization and re-evaluation of the traditional symbolism and ritual scenario. As far as we can judge, the success of the magically oriented wandering cults was due to a certain dissatisfaction with the traditional tribal religion. Moreover, as is clearly shown by the brilliant career of Kuràngara, even if the cult emerged and developed initially in an aboriginal milieu, utilizing exclusively archaic and pan-Australian elements, its popularity and rapid diffusion in later stages are largely due to the consequences of the various tribes' contacts with white man's tools, powers, and beliefs.

[31] *Ibid.*, p. 235; cf. above, pp. 121 ff.

[32] See some examples in Petri, *Sterbende Welt*, pp. 263 ff.

[33] Cf. Petri, "Der australische Medizinmann," Part II, pp. 168 ff. In the early 1930's, Stanner noticed among the Daly River tribes (Northern Territory) a collective neurosis provoked by the terror of *mamakpik*, i.e., the "Devil Doctors," the black magicians par excellence; cf. W. E. H. Stanner, "A Report of Field Work in North Australia: The Daly River Tribes," *Oceania*, IV (1933), esp. 22–25.

Until a few years ago, the only known case of a prophetic millenaristic cult stimulated directly by contact with Western culture was *molonga* or *mulunga*. Having originated in east central Australia and Queensland at the turn of the century, in only a few years *mulunga* reached all the tribes of central and southern Australia. The corroboree lasted five consecutive nights, and many dances portrayed a future war against the whites. At the end appeared Ka'nini, the Spirit of the "Great Mother from the Water," who, in a series of pantomimes, swallowed all the whites.[34] This nativistic and millenaristic cult presents a certain analogy with Kuràngara: the mischievous *mulunga* spirit, just like the Djanba, is invisible to all except the medicine men. But the analogy stops here, for the Djanba are desert spirits, whereas *mulunga* is related to the waters.[35]

In 1960, Helmut Petri and Gisela Petri-Odermann noticed a sort of revivalist movement in the Canning Desert of western Australia, but one lacking prophetic, nativistic, and millenaristic ideas. In 1963, however, the situation was radically changed; the natives refused to accept the two anthropologists again in their traditional ceremonies, and the anti-European feelings were high.[36] The Petris found out

[34] O. Siebert, "Sagen und Sitten der Dieiri und Nachbarr-Stämme in Zentral-Australien," *Globus*, XCVII (1910), 57–59; cf. summary by Petri, "Der australische Medizinmann," Part II, pp. 166–67.

[35] Petri, "Der australische Medizinmann," Part II, p. 167. In his book *Movimenti religiosi di libertà e di salvezza* (Milano, 1960), V. Lanternari included Kuràngara among the prophetic cults (cf. pp. 220 ff.), but he did not discuss the *mulunga*, whose prophetic-millenaristic structure is obvious.

[36] Helmut Petri and Gisela Petri-Odermann, "Nativismus und Millenarismus im gegenwärtigen Australien," *Festschrift für Ad. E.*

from a sympathetic native that a new cult was expected to arrive in the region. They learned that Jinimin (= Jesus) had appeared recently amidst the aborigines. He has black and white skin, and he announced that the entire country will belong to the natives, and also that no distinction will exist between whites and blacks. This will happen only when the natives become powerful enough to conquer the whites. The victory, however, is certain provided the "old law" be faithfully respected. Jesus appears thus as a revivalist prophet of the traditional culture. He is said to have descended from heaven one early afternoon, creating a great surprise. Some people photographed him. He ascended back to heaven at twilight, leaving the Worgaia cult as the means to attain the millennium. Worgaia is a Great Mother type of cult, probably originally from Arnhem Land. Its dynamism was first noticed in 1954.[37]

Another myth from this cult tells of a stone boat sent by Jesus from heaven. The same informants stated definitely that the ship was there from the beginnings of time, from the *bugari-gara*. This is equivalent to saying that Jesus is classified among the mythical Heroes of the tribe. Only as such could he have sent the ship in the primordial time. The ship is invested with two functions: (1) it will serve as Noah's ark when the diluvial rains will kill all the whites with "sacred water"; (2) it is described as loaded with gold and crystals; in other words, it expresses the idea

---

Jensen, II (Munich, 1964), esp. 462. The cause of the change was traced to a white Australian Marxist who had organized a cooperative exclusively for the use of the aborigines. He eventually convinced them to refuse all information to the anthropologists, for they, as a rule, are not sympathetic to the native traditions.

[37] *Ibid.*, p. 464, n. 8.

of the richness of an Australian society that suffered the influence of the white man's economics.[38]

Thus, concluded the Petris, an originally nonaggressive revivalism evolved into an aggressive nativistic and millenaristic cult through a Christian-sectarian reinterpretation. The process took place after the liberalization of official politics with regard to the aborigines and after the aborigines received equal rights with the whites. This indicates that nativistic and millenaristic movements are related more to mystical nostalgias than to purely economic and political circumstances; or, to put it otherwise, it proves how much a politically oriented nativistic movement is permeated with religious symbolism and mystical values.[39]

Though manifestly syncretistic, this new millenaristic cult is grounded essentially in a pan-Australian religious pattern. Jesus is metamorphosed into one of the Culture Heroes of the mythical time, and the strength and ultimate "salvation" of the tribe is declared to be dependent on the respect of tradition. The results of increasing contact with the Western world are therefore not always disruptive of

[38] *Ibid.*, p. 465. Cf. M. Eliade, *Méphistophélès et l'androgyne* (Paris, 1962), pp. 194 ff. (English trans., *Mephistopheles and the Androgyne* [New York, 1965], pp. 155 ff.).

[39] According to a letter of F. Rose, summarized and quoted by the Petris, another movement—of the characteristic cargo type—was noticed at Angas Downs Station, central Australia, in 1962. Here the Americans were to bring trucks loaded with different goods, just as they brought them once during the war. At that time the whites appropriated all these goods by trickery, although they were intended by the Americans to be bestowed upon the natives. Cf. Petri and Petri-Odermann, "Nativismus und Millenarismus," p. 466, n. 10. On the millenaristic motif of the "coming of the Americans," cf. Eliade, *Méphistophélès et l'androgyne*, pp. 155 ff. (English trans., pp. 125 ff.).

traditional values. Moreover, an anti-Western attitude does not necessarily result in pessimism and despair, nor are the purely magical elements inevitably exalted. In sum, the emergence of this cult proves again that future modifications of a "primitive" religion cannot be anticipated. The Australian mind reacts creatively, and therefore diversely, to the challenges raised by acculturation. Even the "political" aspect of some of the new cults represents a creative innovation, being, in fact, a drastic re-evaluation of the traditional understanding of "power."

In all these wandering cults the role of some gifted and dynamic personalities—either medicine men, "black magicians," or "inspired" men and women—seems to have been decisive. The central issue was always a reaction against tradition or a reinterpretation of some of its aspects. As the examples which we discussed illustrate abundantly, even the most violent rejection of the "old law" was expressed in "new" forms that utilized the archaic pan-Australian pattern. The process underlying these radical disruptions and transformations observed in the last sixty to seventy years may help us to understand the less dramatic changes that took place earlier in Australia, as a result of Oceanian and Asian cultural influences.

An "Adjustment Movement"

Creative innovations and unexpected metamorphoses continue to take place under our eyes. In Elcho Island, north of Arnhem Land, about ten years ago, a man named Buramara built a Memorial, a cement-based structure in which the most sacred and secret tribal emblems, the *ranga*, were publicly displayed. Among these *ranga*, until then inaccessible to women and noninitiates, a cross was also exhibited. But Buramara did not intend to Christianize the ancestral religion, although he had his Bible and had been under the influence of missionaries for many years. The "Memorial" cult represents, as Ronald Berndt aptly calls it, an "adjustment movement."[40] At one point Buramara discovered that the *ranga*, which had been photographed by some anthropologists, were being shown to "all the people throughout Australia and other places. . . . We got a shock. We're not supposed to show these *mareeiin*, these *ranga* to just everybody. . . . Then we saw a film at the Elcho church. It was from the American-Australian Expedition, and it showed the sacred ceremonies and emblems. And everybody saw it. . . . We've got no power to hide (these *ranga*): they are taking away our possessions. Are we to lose all this? Our most precious possessions—our *ranga!* We have nothing else: this is really our only wealth" (R. Berndt, *An Adjustment Movement*, p. 40).

According to the aboriginal usage, Buramara thought that if the *ranga* "are shown publicly we should receive something in return" (p. 40). What Buramara and the other leaders of the cult expect from such a revolutionary innovation is first of all a strengthening of the cultural and political unity of the Arnhem Landers. Indeed, the publicly displayed *ranga* express their own "soul," the quintessence of their culture (p. 87). "The Memorial provides a focus and a rallying point" (p. 91). Dressed especially for the occasion and wearing a *ranga* around his forehead, Buramara delivers sermons from a pulpit in front of the Memorial. Traditional singing and dancing take place on the

---

[40] R. M. Berndt, *An Adjustment Movement in Arnhem Land, Northern Territory of Australia* (Paris and The Hague, 1962).

sacred ground. "We have our songs and our dances, said Buramara in one of his sermons, and we do not leave them; we must keep them, since this is the only way to keep us happy. If we drop these it would be very awkward for everybody. . . . Now the missionary here has good news and a good way. We have two minds to think: we worship two Gods. The European Bible is one way: but these *ranga* here on the Memorial are our Bible, and this is not far from the European Bible" (p. 77). As a matter of fact, as Berndt has found it, Christianity as such has not been obtrusive (p. 81).

Thus, it would seem, the history of Australian religions is not yet closed, although the consequences of acculturation may become more and more distressing. One cannot say that the creativity of the Australian religious mind is definitely exhausted or that all that will come from now on will be of only an antiquarian interest.

Historical Reconstruction of Australian Cultures

For more than three-quarters of a century, the Australians have passionately interested anthropologists and sociologists, psychologists and historians of religions.[41] The reasons are obvious: the Australians are food-gatherers and hunters, culturally comparable only with the Fuegians, the Bushmen of the Kalahari desert, and some of the Arctic Eskimos. Thus, one could say that they continue in our days a pre-Neolithic type of culture. Furthermore, the isolation of the continent enhanced the scientific interest in Australian civilization, which was considered to be both

[41] For a review of the earlier interpretations, see D. J. Mulvaney, "The Australian Aborigines 1606–1929: Opinion and Fieldwork," *Historical Studies*, VIII (1958), 131–51, 297–314.

exceptionally archaic and unitary. Explicitly (as in the cases of Frazer, Freud, and Durkheim) or implicitly, scholars were incited by the hope that, through studying the Australians, they would have a chance to discover the "origins" of religious and social institutions.

We know now that such hopes were chimerical. At most, one could say that by studying and understanding the Australians we may grasp the structure and meaning of an archaic type of culture; but this hardly enables us to glimpse the "origins" or the first stages of human culture. Moreover, as recent research abundantly shows, the Australians did not develop—or rather "stagnate"—in a radical isolation, as was thought by Baldwin Spencer and most of his contemporaries. The radio-carbon dates associated unquestionably with human remains are still controversial. According to Gills, the radio-carbon dating of samples from Keilor indicates that they are 18,000 years old; but Abbie thinks that we do not have certain proofs of human remains extending back more than 8,000 years.[42] Mulvaney, however, is inclined to accept Gills's more remote dates;[43] and the linguist Capell, estimating that 8,000 years are insufficient to account for the development of Australian languages suggests "something between 15,000 and 20,000 years."[44]

[42] See W. E. H. Stanner and Helen Sheils (eds.), *Australian Aboriginal Studies: A Symposium of Papers Presented at the 1961 Research Conference* (Melbourne and Oxford, 1963), p. 82.

[43] D. J. Mulvaney, "Prehistory," in *ibid.*, p. 39.

[44] A. A. Capell, summarized in "Discussion on the Antiquity of Man in Australia," in Stanner and Sheils (eds.), *Australian Aboriginal Studies*, p. 84. On the prehistory of Australia, cf. Mulvaney, "Prehistory," pp. 33–51 (select bibliography, 50–51); *idem*, "The Stone Age of Australia," *Proceedings of the Prehistoric Society*,

Whatever the case may be, the sources of Australian civilization lie ultimately in Southeast Asia. McCarthy documented the dependence of Australian prehistoric cultures on Indonesian and Malaysian centers of diffusion, and Tindale supports his conclusions.[45] What is more important, Australia was continually influenced by the flow of culture traits from these areas into Cape York, Arnhem Land, and the Kimberleys. "In other words, the Aborigines' is not an isolated culture which developed independently as is commonly supposed; it is one that has thrived, in a limited manner, on the continuous progress of Oceanic cultures with their roots in Asia. Thus we can distinguish a very large number of customs among all aspects of Aboriginal culture which have an unbroken distribution from Australia into New Guinea and Melanesia, and some further afield. They include customs which are ancient in Australia's cultural terms, and many others of more recent origin which have a limited distribution in the north and east, and which

---

XXVII (1961), 56–107; *idem, The Prehistory of Australia* (London, 1967). See also F. D. McCarthy, "A Comparison of the Prehistory of Australia with That of Indo-China, the Malay Peninsula and Netherlands East Indies," *Proceedings of the Third Congress of Prehistorians of the Far East, Singapore, 1938* (1940), pp. 30–50; *idem, The Stone Implements of Australia* (Sydney, 1946); *idem,* "Recent Developments and Problems in the Prehistory of Australia," *Paideuma*, XIV (1968), 1–16; J. Haekel, "Ethnologische und prähistorische Probleme Australiens," *Wiener völkerkundliche Mitteilungen*, II (1954), 66–85.

[45] McCarthy, "A Comparison of the Prehistory of Australia"; *idem,* "The Oceanic and Indonesian Affiliations of Australian Aboriginal Culture," *Journal of the Polynesian Society*, LXII (1953), 243–61; *idem, Australia's Aborigines: Their Life and Culture* (Melbourne, 1957); N. B. Tindale, "Man of the Hunting Age," *Colorado Quarterly*, VIII (1960), 229–45.

leave no doubt that they were introduced via Cape York whence they spread over the continent."[46] There were long and intimate contacts between the Torres Strait Islanders and the Cape York aborigines. New initiation patterns and Hero cults, together with some technological innovations, arrived from New Guinea and Torres Strait, penetrating the aboriginal culture in Cape York, "where the bow and arrow, skin-drum, and other non-Australian paraphernalia are used" (McCarthy, "The Oceanic and Indonesian Affiliations of Australian Aboriginal Culture," p. 253). The cultural relations between Melanesia and Australia are surprisingly numerous, and have occasioned a large literature.[47] Warner and Berndt have documented Indonesian influences in Arnhem Land,[48] Berndt and McCarthy discovered pottery sherds in northeastern Arnhem Land,[49] and Mulvaney considers it not unlikely that there have been Indonesian Bronze-Iron influences. Indeed, McCarthy had identified a number of typical Bronze Age elements in

[46] McCarthy, "The Oceanic and Indonesian Affiliations of Australian Aboriginal Culture," pp. 243–61, esp. 252 ff. See now *Bolletino del Centro Camuno di Studi Preistorici*, ed. Emmanuel Arati, vol. IV (1968), pp. 111 ff.

[47] See the bibliography in McCarthy, "The Oceanic and Indonesian Affiliations," pp. 253 ff.; cf. also the references listed in the following three notes.

[48] R. M. Berndt, "Discovery of Pottery in North-eastern Arnhem Land," *Journal of the Royal Anthropological Institute*, LXXVII (1947), 133–38; R. M. and C. H. Berndt, *The World of the First Australians*, pp. 20 ff., 424; Warner, *A Black Civilization*, pp. 445 ff.

[49] R. M. Berndt, "Discovery of Pottery in North-eastern Arnhem Land"; F. D. McCarthy and Frank M. Setzler, "The Archeology of Arnhem Land," *Records of the American-Australian Scientific Expedition to Arnhem Land* (1948), II (1960), 223–27.

Australian decorative art (spirals, concentric circles, etc.).[50]

Nevertheless, although Australia has never been "isolated," this does not mean that we must always look outside the continent for explanations of Australian developments. As McCarthy has said:

While Aboriginal culture is not a local Australian phenomenon, neither is its development due solely to outside influences. Davidson presented convincing evidence to show that important modifications, or evolution, of certain artefacts took place in Australia, as for example from the one-piece bark canoe to the pleated and multi-piece sewn types; from emu feather *kurdaitja* shoes to the marsupial, rabbit skin, and bark sandals; from clay skull cap to the use of headnet, separate and dummy mourning caps; and from plain-handled throwing sticks and spearthrowers to those fitted with a gum grip and finally with a stone adze, and the many uses of the spearthrowers in Central Australia. He thus credited the Aborigines with making many intelligent improvements to their artefacts, and in addition pointed out that they had invented or discovered a number of kinds of receptacles by an intelligent exploitation of their resources.[51]

In the discussion following this paper of McCarthy's at the Symposium on Australian Aboriginal Studies (Canberra, May 1961), D. F. Thomson pointed out that the people of Cape York, though familiar with the bow and arrow of the neighboring warlike Torres Strait Islanders, did not borrow them, considering the bow and arrow in-

---

[50] Mulvaney, "Prehistory," p. 50.

[51] F. D. McCarthy, "Ecology, Equipment, Economy and Trade," in Stanner and Sheils (eds.), *Australian Aboriginal Studies*, p. 181. Cf. *ibid.*, p. 188, the bibliography of D. S. Davidson's publications quoted by McCarthy in his paper.

ferior to their fighting spears. Also, "in far north Queensland a gardening culture, familiar to some of the coastal people through contact, was rejected, while some other elements were absorbed and modified or dovetailed into their existing patterns."[52]

Thus, what was once highly esteemed as a static and "monolithic" culture, an expression of a *Naturvolk* living somehow outside history, has proven to be, like all other cultures, "primitive" or highly developed, the result of a historical process. And the fact that the aborigines reacted *creatively* with regard to external cultural influences, accepting and assimilating certain elements, rejecting or ignoring others, shows that they behaved like *historical* beings, and not as a *Naturvolk*. In other words, the historical perspective introduced by prehistorians and historically oriented ethnologists has definitively ruined the image of a stagnant and elementary Australian culture—an image, we may recall, that was successfully popularized by the naturalistic interpretations of nineteenth-century anthropologists.

In fact, the distinctive characteristic of Australians and other primitive peoples is not their lack of history but their specific interpretation of human historicity. They too live in history and are shaped by historical events; but they do not have a historical awareness comparable, say, to that of Westerners; and, because they do not need it, they also lack

[52] D. F. Thomson, summarized in "Discussion," in Stanner and Sheils (eds.), *Australian Aboriginal Studies*, pp. 192–93. The phenomenon is not unparalleled: the Bambuti Pygmies did not borrow plant cultivation from the Bantu agriculturalists, with whom they lived in symbiosis a great number of centuries; cf. P. Schebesta, *Die Bambuti-Pygmäen vom Ituri* (Brussels, 1941), II, 269.

a historiographical consciousness.[53] The aborigines do not record historical exents in an irreversible chronological order. The changes and innovations, which imperceptibly but continuously transformed their existence, were telescoped into the mythical era; that is, they became part of the tribal sacred history. Like most archaic peoples, the Australians do not have any use for *real* chronology. Their sacred history is meaningful, not because it narrates the events in a chronological order, but because it reveals the beginnings of the world, the appearance of the Ancestors, and their dramatic and exemplary deeds.

In conclusion, the reconstruction of the cultural history of the Australians has a great importance for Western scholarship and ultimately for the Western understanding of "primitive" peoples—but it is irrelevant for the aborigines themselves. This means also that the eventual reconstruction of Australian religious history will not necessarily disclose the meaning of the various aboriginal religious creations. Until recently, all innovations and external influences were integrated into a traditional pattern. Finding out that such and such a religious element—a Culture Hero, a myth, a ritual—was introduced rather late, and from a specific region, does not at the same time reveal its significance in the system into which it was integrated. Such external religious elements became part of the traditional mythology, and consequently they demand to be understood and evaluated within that total context. Thus, an historical reconstruction of Australian religions, even accepting that such an enterprise will ever be possible, will not permit the

[53] Cf. M. Eliade, *The Myth of the Eternal Return* (New York: Pantheon, 1954); *idem, Myth and Reality* (New York: Harper & Row, 1963).

scholar to dispense with the hermeneutical work, that is, the *understanding* of the different religious creations whose history he is trying to decipher.

This certainly does not mean that the historical reconstruction is a vain endeavor. As we shall presently see, it was of the utmost importance in proving that circumcision, for example, was introduced rather late into Australia: one recalls the innumerable and extravagant theories, before and after Freud, grounded on the supposed antiquity of circumcision.

Historical Interpretations of Australian Religions

Compared with the results obtained by the specialists in prehistory and historical ethnology, the historical analysis of Australian religious ideas, institutions, and beliefs has marked very little progress. Most probably, the rigidity of the first historical reconstructions, elaborated by Graebner and Wilhelm Schmidt, discouraged the younger generations of scholars from utilizing the same approach.[54] Besides, as we have pointed out,[55] the interests of the scholarly world switched from historical to sociological and psychological analyses and interpretations of primitive religions. Nevertheless, the results of the last thirty years of comparative ethnological research did help to clarify some problems of great interest to the historian of religions. For instance, today no scholar will grant a primary religious importance to circumcision or subincision, rituals that were

---

[54] See the rather melancholic observations of Wilhelm Koppers, "Diffusion: Transmission and Acceptance," in William L. Thomas, Jr. (ed.), *Yearbook of Anthropology* (New York, 1955), pp. 169–81, esp. 171, 178 ff.

[55] Above, pp. 20 ff.

introduced rather late from Melanesia; nor will he consider "totemism" as the basic, universal, and most archaic religious form; furthermore, the fertility cults of Arnhem Land, though representing a characteristic aboriginal religious creation, are the results of Melanesian influences, and as such they cannot throw light on the older pattern of Australian religions. Also, in some cases we are now able to distinguish between chronologically different phases of religious institutions, as, for example, between the simplest forms of puberty initiation and some more elaborated rituals ultimately derived from Melanesia. Moreover, we realize today that megalithic cultures reached Australia a long time ago and have been completely integrated in the religious life of a great number of tribes from Kimberley to Cape York Peninsula.[56]

What results also from recent studies is the surprising diffusion of religious ideas, rituals, and vocabulary throughout the entire continent. In some cases, the dispersion of a religious term in far distant places has posed difficult historical questions. For instance, Father Worms noticed that Bundjil, the name of the highest Being of the Kurnai and other tribes in eastern Victoria, is found in northern Kimberley as *Bundjil miri*, designating the Lord of the Dead, while on the southeastern coast of Carpentaria *bungil* is used for "man," and in the Seymour district the same term means "eaglehawk." Worms remarks: "On reading this we immediately ask ourselves who transported these words? At what time? By what exchange routes over our conti-

---

[56] See, *inter alia*, E. A. Worms, "Contemporary and Prehistoric Rock Paintings in Central and Northern Kimberley," *Anthropos*, L (1955), 546–66, esp. 552 ff.; Gisela Odermann, "Holz- und Steinsetzungen in Australien," *Paideuma*, VII (1959), 99–141.

nent?"[57] It is doubtful that this and other such problems can ever be solved in an historical perspective, for the simple reason that a great number of tribes have disappeared or are hopelessly acculturated.

In spite of the innumerable lacunae in our information, Father Worms was able to present at the Canberra symposium a list of the "essential features" of aboriginal religions and another one of "probable incidental accretions." According to him, the "essential features" are:

1. the absence of esoteric doctrine; 2. belief in a personal sky-being; 3. belief in auxiliary spirit-beings—most often a son of the sky-being—who are the tutors in sacred rites and the donors of sacred instruments; 4. the existence of holy objects left behind by the sky-being, which represent him and contain all his power; 5. the use of liturgical drama to renew and symbolize the creative actions of the being; 6. initiation, excluding corporal operations for both sexes, but including tests of hardship, usually involving plucking of the hair; 7. traces of sacrifice and prayer, in the widest sense of the words; and 8. the existence of a leading liturgist, or medicine man [Worms, "Religion," p. 232].

Among the questions raised by these "essential features," the author asks: "Were essential features originally imported? From where? Which ones? Have others been lost, added to, developed or replaced? Which ones, when, and why?" and so on (p. 233).

In the list of "probable incidental accretions" he includes: "(1) the appearance of secondary beings—ancestors'

[57] E. A. Worms, "Religion," in Stanner and Sheils (eds.), *Australian Aboriginal Studies*, pp. 231–47; cf. esp. p. 236.

spirits, hero spirits—and of wander myths; (2) the introduction of esoteric practices which exclude women; (3)
the appearance of stronger symbolism, especially in regard
to the serpent and other animals; (4) the spread of circumcision and subincision while retaining older and less severe
mutilations (hair-plucking, tooth-cutting, etc.); (5) numerous increase ceremonies, bilocation, thread cross, in-
cantations and the element of fear; (6) second burial,
variation of attitude toward life after death, etc."; and also
(8) the idea of spirit children (pp. 233–34). And the
author asks himself: "When did these and other incidental
accretions in religion commence? Where did they come
from?" and so on (p. 234).

To a certain extent, Father Worms's classification follows that of Father Schmidt, with the difference that
Worm's lists are tentative and are accompanied by a great
number of open questions. Some of the characteristics
enumerated by Father Worms seem plausible. As a matter
of fact, most of the "essential features" may have belonged
to the archaic stages of Australian religions. Furthermore,
a number of "probable incidental accretions" (such as the
spread of circumcision and subincision, the introduction of
esoteric practices, etc.) most probably do represent late
developments. But how can one prove that "numerous increase ceremonies," or "the element of fear," or "variations
of attitude towards life after death," or the idea of spirit
children are "incidental accretions"? Such beliefs, rites, and
ideas could have accompanied the "essential features" from
the very beginnings of Australian religions—which, let us
repeat, are not to be confused with the "beginnings" of
religion.

Anthropologists and Australian Religions

Father Worms's synthetical sketch seems to be the latest effort to present an all-encompassing view of Australian religions, analyzed both morphologically and historically. Neither in the discussion which followed his paper nor elsewhere in the most recent ethnological literature, has such a "total" approach—his heritage from Graebner, Schmidt, and the Vienna School—aroused a real interest among scholars. On the contrary, as is well known, the Australian ethnologists, especially Elkin and his disciples and younger colleagues, have concentrated on monographical studies and morphological analyses of different religious forms and systems.[58] Moreover, Elkin, the Berndts, and Stanner have also published general presentations of the Australian religions. Stanner's methodological approach is particularly encouraging for the historian of religions. The eminent anthropologist emphatically asserts that Australian religion must be studied "*as* religion and not as a mirror of something else."[59] He protests against the general notion that a study of totemism, magic, and ritual exhausts the understanding of a primitive religion. He equally rejects the conviction that the true aim of a real scientific study of religion is to discover "the effect *in* religion of some set of social or psychological variables" (Stanner, *On Aboriginal*

[58] This does not mean, of course, that the contributions of non-Australian ethnologists are less important. A case in point is a recent article by Helmut Petri, "Kosmogonie unter farbigen Völkern der Westlichen Wüste Australiens," *Anthropos,* LX (1965), 469–79. The author discovered a cosmogony up to now unknown, explaining the creation of the world in *four* stages or epochs; see esp. p. 478.

[59] W. E. H. Stanner, *On Aboriginal Religion* ("Oceania Monographs," No. 11 [Sidney, 1963]), p. vi.

Religion, p. vi). In his monograph, Stanner repeatedly criticizes the fallacious presupposition "that the social order is primary and in some sense causal, and the religious order secondary and in some sense consequential. Thus, studies may issue in general propositions to the effect that religion 'reflects' or 'expresses' the social structure. It is quite difficult to see why such statements seem important or even interesting. They are not clear even as metaphor" (p. 27).

The particular tribe studied by Stanner is the Murinbata, in the northwestern parts of the Arnhem territory, but the author aims at disclosing a structure of meaning valid for other Australian religions as well. One of the most unexpected results of his analysis regards the initiation ceremony Punj or Karwadi. Stanner convincingly shows that this ceremony bears a marked resemblance to sacrifice (pp. 25 ff). The studies consecrated to symbolism, myth, and ritual (pp. 60–132) abound in new and fruitful ideas. The decisive role Stanner sees in the myths depicting the "foundations" of the world will meet with the total agreement of the historian of religions.[60] The Murinbata thought that they could understand the dramas which took place in the mythical time; they recognized in their countryside the concrete traces of those mythical events, and they asserted that they were "connected intimately—as individuals, sexes, genetic stocks, groups and categories—with personages, places and events of the dramas" (p. 152). In the primordial times the "two domains of life became distinct but remained co-existent and interdependent. There were then, and are now, an incorporeal (but not necessarily invisible) domain, and a corporeal (but not necessarily visible) do-

[60] *Ibid.,* pp. 152, 164, etc. Cf. above, Chapter 2.

main. The former has the greater power" (p. 153). The main rites reactualize the creative elements of the primordial times. "Each ritual occasion vivified in the minds of celebrants the first instituting of the culture, deepened the sense of continuity with men's beginnings, and reaffirmed the structures of existence" (*ibid.*). In concluding, Stanner deplores that "it is not seen clearly enough that totems and social situations simply provided familiar, convenient symbols by which to adumbrate what could not be designated more sharply or succinctly: that is, the things of ultimate religious concern."[61]

It was not in our intentions to summarize this rich, profound, and stimulating monograph. But it is important to point out the radical change in the anthropologist's understanding of Australian religion that is illustrated by Stanner's work. In the first chapter[62] we made an allusion to the rather unfortunate consequences of the vogue of totemism, launched by Durkheim's *Formes élémentaires,* and of the hypothesis of the primitives' *mentalité prélogique* elaborated by Lévy-Bruhl. Both interpretations were antihistorical and reductionistic ("sociologism" and "psychologism"). Half a century later, Stanner comes to these conclusions; "(1) If any Australian aborigines lived, as used to be suggested, in a stationary state of society with a static culture, the Murinbata were certainly not among them over any period which it is possible for inquiry to touch. (2) To identify their religion with totemic phenomena would be a mistake. (3) The society was not the real source and object of the religion" (p. 154).

[61] Stanner, *On Aboriginal Religion,* p. 154. See also the conclusions, pp. 165–71.

[62] Above, pp. 20 ff.

Developing and generalizing some remarks of Van Gennep and Radcliffe-Brown, Claude Lévi-Strauss has brilliantly criticized what he has called the "totemic illusion."[63] There is no specific and unitary type of religion called "totemism." For Lévi-Strauss, "the totemic representations amount to a code which make it possible to pass from one system to another regardless of whether it is formulated in natural or cultural terms."[64] We shall have to discuss elsewhere Lévi-Strauss's general interpretation of mythical thinking. The model of his structuralist approach is inspired by structural linguistics, especially phonology. Paul Ricoeur and Jean Hypolithe have noticed with regard to *Le Pensée sauvage* that Lévi-Strauss is interested in a *syntax*, and not in a *semantics*, of myth. On the other hand, in many passages of *La Pensée sauvage* the author does not limit himself to the operation of decoding systems of classifications and multiple relations but brilliantly analyzes specific Australian cultural creations, related to a particular mode of existing in the world. Thus, Lévi-Strauss seems

[63] See Claude Lévi-Strauss, *Le Totémisme aujourd'hui* (Paris, 1962), esp. pp. 21 ff. (English trans., *Totemism* [Boston, 1963], pp. 15 ff.); *idem*, *La Pensée sauvage* (Paris, 1962), pp. 48 ff., 100 ff., and *passim* (English trans., *The Savage Mind* [Chicago, 1966], pp. 35 ff., 75 ff., and *passim*).

[64] *The Savage Mind*, pp. 96–97 (*La Pensée sauvage*, p. 128). "Totemism postulates a logical equivalence between a society of natural species and a world of social groups" (*The Savage Mind*, p. 104; *Le Pensée sauvage*, p. 138). Cf. also *The Savage Mind*, pp. 135 ff. Ethnologists of different schools have expressed comparable views; for instance, Ad. E. Jensen: "Totemistic relationships are only a part of a ramified system which enters into many departments of culture, of which the social order is but one" (*Myth and Cult among Primitive Peoples* [Chicago, 1963], p. 152). The German edition was published in 1951.

equally interested in "semantics." Besides, nothing prevents a structuralist from enlarging his linguistic model, in other words, from carrying out his analysis on the level of the discourse.

It is as yet too soon to evaluate the structuralists' contribution to the understanding of religion, and especially to the understanding of the innumerable forms and aspects of *religious creativity*, such as they appear in the flowing of time, in history. And this is of a paramount importance; for the ultimate goal of the historian of religions is not to point out that there exist a certain number of types or patterns of religious behavior, with their specific symbologies and theologies, but rather to *understand their meanings*. And such meanings are not *given* once and for all, are not "petrified" in the irrespective religious patterns, but rather are "open," in the sense that they change, grow, and enrich themselves in a creative way in the process of history (even if "history" is not apprehended in the Judeo-Christian or modern Western sense). Ultimately, the historian of religions cannot renounce hermeneutics.

Index

201

Australian Religions: An Introduction

Designed by R. E. Rosenbaum.
Composed by York Composition Co., Inc.
in 11 point linotype Janson, 3 points leaded,
with display lines in Helvetica.
Printed letterpress from type by York Composition Co., Inc.
on Warren's No. 66 text, 60 pound basis,
with the Cornell University Press watermark.
Bound by Vail-Ballou Press
in Columbia book cloth
and stamped in All Purpose foil.

Library of Congress Cataloging in Publication Data
(For library cataloging purposes only)

Eliade, Mircea, date.
  Australian religions.

  (Symbol, myth, and ritual series)
  Based on a course delivered by the author at the University of Chicago, 1964. The pref. first appeared in 1967 as On understanding primitive religions, in Glaube und Geschichte, Festschrift für Ernst Benz; the
remainder of the book is reprinted from History of religions, v. 6–7
(1966–67)
  Includes bibliographical references.
  1. Australia—Religion. 2. Mythology, Australian
(Aboriginal) I. Title.
BL2610.E44   299'.9   72-6473
ISBN 0-8014-0729-X